THE
NARCISSIST
YOU KNOW

JOSEPH BURGO, PhD

Touchstone
New York   London   Toronto   Sydney   New Delhi

Touchstone
An Imprint of Simon & Schuster, Inc.
1230 Avenue of the Americas
New York, NY 10020

First Touchstone paperback edition September 2016

TOUCHSTONE and colophon are registered trademarks of Simon & Schuster, Inc.

For information about special discounts for bulk purchases, please contact Simon & Schuster Special Sales at 1-866-506-1949 or business@simonandschuster.com.

The Simon & Schuster Speakers Bureau can bring authors to your live event. For more information or to book an event contact the Simon & Schuster Speakers Bureau at 866-248-3049 or visit our website at www.simonspeakers.com.

Interior design by Jill Putorti

Manufactured in the United States of America

10 9 8 7 6 5

The Library of Congress has cataloged the hardcover edition as follows:

Burgo, Joseph (Psychologist)
    The narcissist you know / by Joseph Burgo.
       pages   cm
    1. Narcissism.   I. Title.
    BF575.N35B87   2015
    155.2'32—dc23   2015003423

ISBN 978-1-4767-8568-4
ISBN 978-1-4767-8569-1 (pbk)
ISBN 978-1-4767-8570-7 (ebook)

For Michael

TABLE OF CONTENTS

Table of Contents

INTRODUCTION

In recent years, overuse of the word "narcissism" has stripped away much of its weight and import. In today's selfie-obsessed, social-media–driven culture, narcissism has become more or less synonymous with "vanity."

Referring to someone as a "narcissist" has become the favorite lay diagnosis du jour of pundits and commentators who eagerly apply it to the latest celebrity engulfed in scandal or the politician caught in bad behavior. Most people use it as an insult or a put-down, a way to deflate others when they seem too self-important. We apply it to men and women across the social spectrum, from famous actors who misbehave in the public spotlight to friends who constantly post flattering photos of themselves on Instagram.

These days, it seems that almost everyone is narcissistic.

When a label applies to that many people, its meaning becomes diffuse and overgeneralized. Referring to someone as a "narcissist" has become cliché, so common that we no longer think about what it actually means.

This book aims to rescue narcissism from trivialization and to shed light on its complex nature. Narcissism exists along a continuum of possible expressions, from healthy self-regard on one end to pathological narcissism on the other. In Chapter One, we'll explore the traits of Narcissistic Personality Disorder as defined by the American Psychiatric Association (a clinical diagnosis that applies to only 1 percent of the general population), but most of the book will focus on those people I refer to as "Extreme Narcissists."

They make up an astounding 5 percent of the population.

They fall short of the diagnostic threshold for Narcissistic Personality Disorder but they also differ in important ways from run-of-the-mill narcissists who think a little too well of themselves.

Extreme Narcissists are not just vain and irritating . . . they're dangerous.

PSYCHOLOGICAL MEANING VS. DIAGNOSIS

This is not a book about diagnosis. I see little value in attaching diagnostic labels when doing so reduces complex individuality to a stereotype. It tells us nothing useful about *why* Extreme Narcissists act the way they do, or the psychic pain that lies behind their more destructive and often deliberately hurtful behavior.

In the pages ahead, you'll learn to spot Extreme Narcissists among your friends, family, and co-workers, and you'll come to understand what drives them. Along the way, you'll also learn some useful ways of coping with the Extreme Narcissist you know. Once you recognize narcissistic behavior in others and how it affects your own psyche, you'll be able to avoid inciting its most noxious expressions. You can develop effective ways of responding to the Extreme Narcissists in your life without wounding their fragile sense of self or reacting in ways that only provoke them further.

I hope you'll also learn something about yourself in the process—how your defensive reactions make you an occasional narcissist. You'll learn how to recognize and restrain those narcissistic tendencies we all exhibit from time to time, especially the ones that disrupt our personal lives and cause trouble in our relationships.

THE NARCISSISTS I DON'T KNOW

Throughout this book, I discuss real-life examples of people who exemplify the traits of Extreme Narcissism, and some of them are well-known celebrities. Whenever I write about a famous athlete such as Lance Armstrong or a politician like Eliot Spitzer, using their life stories as a way to shed light on the psychology of narcissism, a disgruntled reader or two will usually ask how I "presume" to diagnose a person I've never met.

I have a simple answer to this question: I don't presume to diagnose *anyone*, much less a stranger. I've never seen much value in diagnostic labels.

On the other hand, although I would never presume to diagnose someone I haven't met, I do know narcissism when I see it, even from a distance. I've been treating, reading, and writing about narcissism throughout a lengthy career. During and after my personal analysis, I spent many years coming to terms with my own narcissism and what lies behind it. Thanks to clients who have entrusted themselves to my care, I've had the opportunity to explore the myriad expressions of their narcissism, coming to understand the way it functions as a defense against pain, although that pain is often invisible.

Empathizing with my clients' pain is at the core of the work I do and the only way I can fully understand what drives their narcissistic behavior. In the pages ahead, I'll describe many of those clients and what I learned from them. (Personal characteristics and the details of their lives have of course been changed to obscure their identities.) Though I haven't actually met any of the public figures I'll be discussing, I've tried to empathize with them all the same, finding a way into their pain by closely reading the work of excellent biographers such as Walter Isaacson and J. Randy Taraborrelli.

In the process, I've spent long hours trying to understand famous people whose behavior can be deeply offensive. With each of them, I've managed to find at least one moment in their lives when their suffering became clear to me. In the course of describing their often brutal behavior—the vindictive ways they treated people close to them and the hurt they deliberately inflicted—I've tried to keep that moment in mind.

Narcissists are notoriously lacking in empathy; if we simply judge them, heaping scorn and derision upon their offensive behavior, we have merely responded in kind. I invite you to join with me in my effort to feel empathy rather than to judge. Whether they show it or even realize it themselves, Extreme Narcissists are always in flight from pain. Try to remember this fact as you read ahead.

In a way, it may actually be easier for you to empathize with celebrity narcissists, strangers viewed from a safe distance, because you don't have to interact with them. You don't have to endure their hostility and contempt, or live in fear of retaliation for your unintended slight. The Extreme Narcissists you know personally present a much greater challenge, for despite your best efforts to protect yourself or to mollify their pride, you may find yourself a target. Some narcissists are merely self-absorbed and socially tone-deaf, but others are dangerous. Not only do they cause personal, professional, and financial havoc in your life, they often attack your self-esteem. The more influence they wield in your life, the greater their power to affect how you feel about yourself.

When the Extreme Narcissist you know behaves as if you are stupid, inferior, and contemptible, you will likely feel hurt or angry, and it may sound like a superhuman challenge to empathize with someone who is attacking you. An intellectual understanding may be all you can manage, but it's what you need to strive for, rather than mounting a counterassault to protect yourself and give voice to your anger. As I'll show, managing an Extreme Narcissist depends largely on mastering *your own* reactions to their behavior, *your own* defensive responses to their assaults on your self-esteem. A central theme of this book is that coping effectively with the narcissist you know often means coming to terms with your own narcissism.

In writing this book, I've avoided theory and technical jargon, striving instead for the everyday language of emotion—the way you and I talk about our feelings when we're among friends. There are few references to the many important theorists who have written about narcissism and whose views have influenced my own, but readers who would like to know more about those theories will find a list of suggested readings at the end of the book. For an overview of the most important theories about narcissism and how they relate to one another, I particularly recommend Andrew Morrison's excellent book on the subject.

But I don't believe you need to master the intricacies of psychoanalytic theory in order to understand narcissism. At heart, Extreme Narcissists fear that they are frauds, that they will be exposed as small, ugly, defective, or without value. They constantly strive to come across as "winners" because they fear that they are actually "losers" instead. The ineluctable bond between would-be winners and the losers they despise lies at the heart of Extreme Narcissism.

And that is something I believe everyone can understand.

"I HAVE MANY DIFFERENT FACES"

The Narcissistic Continuum

Sam's earliest memories involve his parents' epic fights—voices raised, plates flying, tears and recriminations that sometimes ended in physical violence. His father would accuse his mother of infidelity, while she railed about his emotional neglect. Not long after Sam turned six, his parents divorced. During the ensuing years, he rarely saw his father, who remarried and started a second family. In the meantime, a long string of men, his mother's boyfriends, moved in and out of Sam's life. Most of them had a hard time coping with the boy's defiant, hostile attitude. A few of them felt provoked enough to beat him. His mother never remarried.

During middle school, Sam was fairly popular and an A student, though extremely intolerant of criticism. He frequently wound up in the principal's office for overly aggressive behavior. Even back then, before the antibullying campaign had gathered steam, his persecution of the shy and the weak regularly brought reprimands. In high school, he directed his immense competitive energy into athletics and eventually became captain of the football team, despite clashes with his coach over his disrespect and "glory hogging." The coach knew his star player needed a strong paternal hand to help him manage that tormented, angry drive of his, but Sam rebuffed him. "You're not my dad!" he snarled on more than one occasion. Eventually Sam received an athletic scholarship to Stanford and was recruited by Exxon upon graduation.

As a rising corporate executive, Sam was a fierce competitor, relentless in his drive to succeed, cocky and self-confident in a way that some colleagues found charming, others abrasive. He had no close friends and viewed other people with suspicion: From his cynical perspective, everyone in life was "playing an angle." When necessary, he could feign deference toward his superiors, concealing his contempt and the immense envy he felt for their wealth and power. Rising through the ranks, he demanded complete and uncritical loyalty from his own subordinates. If they complied, he generously rewarded them. But if a member of his team failed to live up to his expectations, Sam would cast that person aside without regret. Over time, he gathered around him a devoted group of hardworking men and women who both admired and feared him.

His personal life was marked by the same competitive drive, demands for loyalty, and abrupt dismissals of those who disappointed him. After a long string of one-night stands and short-term relationships, Sam fell headlong in love with Miranda, a top runway model, whom he adored with idealistic passion. Once married, she gave up her career at his insistence. He then built them a showplace pointedly larger than the homes owned by his fellow corporate officers. They began to collect art and build a wine cellar. Sam and Miranda hosted lavish parties and elegant dinners, over which he presided with a kind of dictatorial charm.

As Miranda aged, Sam's passion for her gradually cooled. When she became pregnant and "lost her figure," he made snide comments and started an affair with one of his subordinates. Sam and Miranda had two sons, whom he loved in an authentic but limited way, seeing them more as reflections upon himself than as truly separate people. As a parent, he was perfectionistic and demanding but only intermittently focused on his children's activities. He forgot school plays and athletic events he had promised to attend. He made sure his boys went to the most expensive private schools but never attended a single parent-teacher conference.

Though not an introspective man, Sam occasionally had his dark moments when he felt alone and uncared for, surrounded by hungry mouths he had to feed, literally and figuratively, or besieged by up-and-coming competitors who wanted his job. The world sometimes struck him as a hostile place, beset with dangers. At those moments, an angry sort of self-pity could set in. If it weren't for his power and money, would anyone give a damn what happened to him? Even his own mother, sunk deep into alcoholism by that time, was always hitting him up for another "loan."

As he reached the pinnacle of his career, Sam traveled the world extensively on the corporate jet, usually in the company of one of his mistresses. Whenever Miranda or the children complained about his absence, he called them ungrateful for failing to appreciate the affluent lifestyle he afforded them. Miranda eventually filed for divorce. Incensed, Sam hired a lawyer known for his slash-and-burn tactics, who so relentlessly persecuted Miranda that she finally gave up, walking away from the marriage with very little. Sam spread vicious rumors about her within their social set, telling unfounded tales about her promiscuity and drug abuse. Using his wealth as a weapon, he attempted to lure their children away from Miranda, threatening to cut them off if they didn't take his side.

Sam perfectly fits the profile for Narcissistic Personality Disorder (NPD), a favorite diagnosis regularly made by reporters, bloggers, and professional psychologists opining in the public sphere. While the label is sometimes used loosely, with commentators applying the term "narcissistic" to just about anyone deemed conceited or overly focused on garnering attention, the American Psychiatric Association (APA) actually has precise criteria for Narcissistic Personality Disorder that are codified in its "bible"—the *Diagnostic and Statistical Manual for Mental Disorders* (or the DSM).

So who qualifies as an "official" narcissist? According to the DSM, a person must demonstrate at least five of the following features to receive this diagnosis:

- A grandiose sense of self-importance—in other words, the individual exaggerates achievements and talents and expects to be recognized as superior without commensurate achievements
- A preoccupation with fantasies of unlimited success, power, brilliance, beauty, or ideal love
- A belief that he or she is special and unique and can only be understood by, or should associate with, other special or high-status people (or institutions)

- A need for excessive admiration
- A sense of entitlement—unreasonable expectations of especially favorable treatment or automatic compliance with his or her expectations
- Interpersonally exploitative behavior—someone who takes advantage of others to achieve his or her own ends
- A lack of empathy—a person who is unwilling to recognize or identify with the feelings and needs of others
- Envy of others or a belief that others are envious of him or her
- A demonstration of arrogant and haughty behaviors or attitudes

Going by this strict definition, Sam definitely meets the diagnostic criteria for Narcissistic Personality Disorder. He displays an obvious lack of empathy; he is preoccupied with enormous success and needs uncritical admiration; he's arrogant, envious, and grandiose, and he ruthlessly exploits other people. In fact, Sam demonstrates more than five of the nine diagnostic criteria for Narcissistic Personality Disorder, which points unambiguously toward this diagnosis.

But you probably could have made this diagnosis yourself, just by reading his story. Sam's case isn't particularly nuanced, and though you may not know someone like Sam firsthand, you've probably seen similar behavior in the escapades of high-flying politicians, actors, or business titans. He's a classic case of Narcissistic Personality Disorder.

But what about the other narcissists who are all around us? What about those people who fall short of the diagnostic criteria for NPD but aren't simply vain or conceited?

NARCISSISM EXISTS ON A SPECTRUM

Since the first edition of the DSM was published in 1952, psychological thought and science has undergone several revolutions . . . and the book itself has undergone several revisions, too. In early editions, Freudian theory reigned supreme. Narcissistic tendencies were attributed to our early experiences with our mother or father, and the cure would be psychoanalysis, and lots of it.

But beginning around 1974, Freudian theory waned in influence and a more "scientific" orientation came to dominate the DSM. As the pendulum swung, the APA's diagnosis manual began to adopt a disease model of mental illness, where psychological disorders are largely viewed as a medical condition, one that can be cured by a pill rather than by talk therapy. With its symptom checklist and elaborate numeric codes, the most recent edition (DSM5) strives to identify psychological conditions that are as discrete and circumscribed as any physical illness, such as glaucoma or asthma.

There are many positive effects of this shift—and viewing psychological problems as diseases rather than as moral failings has gone a long way to alleviate the stigma associated with mental illness. At the same time, the APA has taught us to view many disorders as the result of chemical imbalances or genetic defects, without exploring the *meaning* of their symptoms or their roots in personal history.

Low levels of serotonin in your brain are the cause of your depression, patients are told. *This pill will take care of it.*

This prevailing view of mental illness is not only misleading, it's dangerous. It focuses on extreme cases that fit a clinical definition without providing guidance for how to spot and cope with lesser though often serious expressions of a disorder. Narcissism isn't a disease that you can turn off or on with a pill. Remember that nine-point narcissism checklist from the DSM? Sam would be diagnosed with Narcissistic Personality Disorder because he met five of the nine criteria. What if he only met four of them? Or what if his ability to empathize were *severely limited* rather than entirely absent?

Some men and women barely reach the diagnostic threshold for NPD. Others fall just short. A great many other people more closely fit another diagnosis but at the same time seem quite *narcissistic*. These people could be just as troubled, and just as destructive to themselves and those around them . . . and it can be difficult to get them the help they need because they don't fit some rigid definition in the DSM.

In fact, narcissism exists in many shades and degrees of severity along a continuum, as do many other high-profile medical and psychological conditions, like autism or bipolar disorder. In order to understand narcissism—to make sense of the narcissists we all know and to find ways of coping with them—we need to look beyond its strict definition in the DSM. To see people like Sam as afflicted with a disease sets them apart, as if they have nothing to do with our own emotional experience and are therefore incomprehensible. But as I'll show in the pages ahead, the narcissistic features they display are actually the most extreme form of traits that show up across the spectrum of mental disorders, and more mildly in the general population.

In short, narcissism is a universal aspect of human psychology, existing along a continuum of possible expressions.

Although the APA sets forth nine potential criteria for Narcissistic Personality Disorder—as if they were distinct disease traits as well defined as the fatigue and shortness of breath that often characterize anemia—those nine features actually overlap and interconnect. From a psychological perspective, where symptoms have *meaning*, those nine actually boil down to two: an inflated sense of self-importance and a lack of empathy for other people; the remaining features are by-products that naturally follow from them.

A person with a grandiose sense of self would likely believe herself to be unique, part of a superior elite and destined for greatness. She would feel entitled to special treatment, coming across as arrogant or haughty, and expect others to admire her. Someone who lacks empathy would more readily exploit other people for personal gain, or envy them for the simple reason that they possess what she wants.

An inflated sense of self-importance and *a lack of empathy for other people:* As I'll be discussing throughout this book, these two psychological traits lie at the heart of narcissism. They largely define Narcissistic Personality Disorder according to the APA, but they often show up in other psychological disorders as well. An inflated sense of self-importance characterizes mania and the manic phases of bipolar disorder. "Ideas of reference" that show up in paranoia, and various psychotic disorders, organize the universe around the self; other people become two-dimensional enemies, characters in one's personal drama, with no authentic interior life of their own. People who struggle with manic-depressive illness have little emotional room left over for other people.

In other words, many individuals who don't meet the full diagnostic criteria for Narcissistic Personality Disorder are narcissists all the same—Extreme Narcissists, as I refer to them. And they are all around us, causing us damage, wreaking havoc in our lives. We're ill equipped to cope with them. Often we don't even spot them until it's too late.

Consider the case of Naomi.

THE NARCISSIST NEXT DOOR

People who don't know her well often describe Naomi in saintly terms. In addition to her work as a kindergarten teacher, she organizes fund-raising drives for breast cancer research and takes an active part in her congregation's outreach to the underprivileged. At Christmas, she coordinates a gift-giving program with her local social services department, making sure that all children in foster care receive every item on their Christmas wish lists. Twice a month, she volunteers for the hot line sponsored by a shelter for battered women in her community.

"What this world needs," acquaintances often tell her, "is more people like you."

Naomi's three adult children have a very different view of her. "Mother is *difficult*," they often say. It's hard to know in advance what will set her off, but certain subjects are clearly dangerous. They learned long ago never to contradict their mother when she vilifies her ex-husband, painting herself as a long-suffering martyr abandoned by a heartless philanderer who left in search of younger flesh. They never mention contacts with their father and lie point-blank if Naomi asks whether they've seen him. Melissa, the youngest, once made the mistake of showing off an expensive watch she received from him on her birthday. Naomi acted deeply wounded and turned chilly toward Melissa, launching small digs and snide remarks for weeks thereafter.

Naomi tends to play rotating favorites. Sometimes Molly is the good girl and her sister, Melissa, the problem; then they'll switch roles following some unintended slight to Naomi's self-regard. Their brother, Josh, the golden child, her pride and joy, seems largely immune from criticism. It helps that he's a successful surgeon with a large home in the finest part of town. He buys his mother a new car every few years and occasionally sends her on a Mediterranean cruise. At work, Naomi goes on and on to her colleagues about her dutiful, generous, loving, successful, and wealthy son. How he dotes on her!

If the two sisters have lunch alone, or all three siblings get together without inviting Naomi, they know better than to mention it: She'd feel left out and jealous. "Once her children are grown," Naomi often says in martyred tones, "a mother just doesn't matter." However, at full family gatherings, she still makes herself the center of attention. When Melissa or Josh asks about Molly's job at the local public TV station, Naomi soon forces her way back into the spotlight with well-worn subject changers: "That reminds me of the time . . ." or "Speaking of such-and-such, did I ever tell you about . . ."

Whenever events take a turn for the worse in the lives of her children, Naomi can be lavish in her sympathy. Molly once contracted a staph infection while in the hospital for gallbladder surgery, and Naomi visited her every day, preparing casseroles for Molly's family so "they wouldn't starve." When Melissa lost her job, Naomi stepped forward with financial support and a great deal of advice. But if good fortune should come their way, she offers rote congratulations and lapses into silence. The day Molly won an award for a documentary she produced at the station, Naomi took to bed with a mysterious ailment the doctors could never explain.

Naomi doesn't meet the diagnostic criteria for Narcissistic Personality Disorder, though she does display an inflated sense of self-importance and limited empathy for the members of her family. She's neither grandiose nor preoccupied by fantasies of unlimited success, power, beauty, et cetera. Although emotionally manipulative, she doesn't actually exploit other people for personal gain. She's neither arrogant nor haughty. Of the nine diagnostic criteria listed in the DSM, she demonstrates three or four at most.

And yet Naomi is undoubtedly an Extreme Narcissist. She may not be as blatantly narcissistic as Sam, but, psychologically speaking, these two people have a lot in common. And both are destructive forces in the lives of those around them. Extreme Narcissists are people whose inflated sense of self-importance and limited empathy bring pain and turmoil to their friends, family members, and acquaintances.

Odds are you don't personally know people like Sam, though you might have seen their names in the headlines or heard about them on the news: politicians, athletes, or entertainers whose careers have dramatically collapsed before the public eye following some scandal—the Anthony Weiners, Eliot Spitzers, and Arnold Schwarzeneggers of the world. They dominate the realm of celebrity, where the personality traits expressed in Extreme Narcissism prove useful as they claw their way to the top.

Until recently, Narcissistic Personality Disorder was believed to show up in about 1 percent of the population, or one in a hundred people, most of them men, but the latest studies point to a much larger number. Many of them have learned to disguise their socially unacceptable traits in order to control the impression they make and to better manipulate people. On a casual level, they can appear quite charming, so unless you get to know them well, you might never realize you're dealing with a diagnosable narcissist according to the DSM.

But as a character trait rather than a discrete diagnostic category, narcissism shows up not only in the other personality disorders but across the spectrum of psychological illness, affecting as much as

5 percent of the population, women as well as men. In all walks of life, we meet the Extreme Narcissist on a regular basis. It might be your boss or a colleague at work. Your sister-in-law. That new person you're dating or a member of your social group.

Many people think better of themselves than they actually deserve—men and women with no obvious psychological disorder but whose personality and behavior make them seem narcissistic. Self-centered or preoccupied with their own image, they're fairly insensitive to the feelings of other people, though not entirely lacking in empathy. They're often envious or jealous people who easily take offense. They may dominate conversation at dinner parties or make themselves the center of attention in large groups. They show limited interest in others and don't usually recognize when they've hurt someone's feelings. Less obviously narcissistic than Sam or even Naomi, and far from meeting the criteria for NPD, they are Extreme Narcissists all the same, at least some of the time.

Extreme Narcissists are all around us. They hurt us. They stir up trouble in our relationships with other people. We're ill equipped to handle them because we don't understand what makes them behave in the destructive ways they do.

It helps to know that all of the Extreme Narcissists you'll meet in the pages ahead are trying to feel good about themselves, to prove that they have value, but they often do so in ways that make it difficult to feel any compassion for them. Usually, we can't see what drives their behavior, in particular the unconscious shame that shapes their personalities. The Extreme Narcissist is in flight from himself, and most of what he says and does is an effort to disprove what he unconsciously fears is true—that he is small, defective, and without value.

"I Have Many Different Faces": The Narcissistic Continuum

As the profiles throughout this book will make clear, narcissism exists along a continuum of possible expressions. Sam, who meets the criteria for NPD, stands at one end of that continuum. In the pages ahead, I'll be discussing other men and women who resemble Sam, among them the well-known athletes, politicians, and entertainers whose narcissistic behavior has garnered headlines; but Extreme Narcissists like Naomi are the primary focus of this book—people closer to the middle of our continuum, who fall just short of meeting the criteria for a severe clinical diagnosis, many of them clients from my practice or people they have known.

Before concluding this chapter, however, I'd like to introduce you to one more narcissist.

Me.

THE NARCISSIST IN THE MIRROR

Let me tell you a story about my own narcissistic behavior one day at my piano lesson.

I'd been studying with my teacher, Pei Fen, for more than four years at that point. My oldest son, William, had studied with her for two years before that, so we'd known each other for six or seven years. She's a friend, as well as my teacher: In addition to the playing and instruction that goes on during our lessons, we also talk about our personal lives. Following her annual break during July and August that year, I went to my first lesson with a lot to tell her about my own difficult summer.

In addition to a highly stressful trip to Chicago for William's graduation from college, I also had to cope with an unexpected and upsetting family crisis. The weather had been lousy all summer, and too many houseguests had come to visit, stretching my emotional resources as gracious host, though they were all loved and welcome. I was also worried about Will's depressed state of mind following graduation. Because Pei Fen had known him since he was fifteen years old, I told her all about his graduation and my concerns. I talked about the bad weather and the parade of houseguests and my family emergency. I went on at length. I didn't realize it beforehand, but I think I'd been looking forward to sharing my experience with her, unburdening myself in a way.

We eventually turned to the music, and I was about halfway through the opening theme in my Chopin piece when I realized with a feeling of shame that I hadn't asked Pei Fen a single question about her summer. I'd been so immersed in my own concerns, so wrapped up in my personal universe, where I was of paramount importance, that I briefly lost sight of Pei Fen as a separate person and not merely a friendly ear. I stopped playing and told her, "I was so self-absorbed that I didn't even ask about *you*." It turns out she'd had a serious wrist injury early in July, which meant the cancellation of her summer concerts in Europe, and she was deeply anxious about her upcoming visit to an eminent surgeon.

My point in telling this somewhat embarrassing story is that at times, we are *all* narcissistic. Whenever we're deeply stressed, emotionally thin, or overwhelmed by need, other people may temporarily drop off our emotional radar. If we're caught up in pursuing some goal that matters deeply to us, we might lose touch with the empathy we normally feel. And when our pride receives a blow, we may try to shore up our self-image in ways not so different from the defensive strategies used by the Extreme Narcissists described in the pages ahead.

I have no doubt that you, too, are an occasional narcissist, just like me.

In the coming chapters, I'll explore narcissism in many forms, all along the continuum, from clients in my practice to more visible, well-known celebrities and the Extreme Narcissism they display—the bullying narcissism of Lance Armstrong, for example, or the self-righteous narcissism of Donald Trump. But first, we'll take a look at *narcissistic injury*—the occasional blow to our self-esteem that we all experience from time to time—and what it reveals about the inner world of the Extreme Narcissists you may know. I believe that understanding our own narcissistic tendencies is the best place to begin an exploration of the more pathological forms of narcissism.

"I'M EASILY WOUNDED"

Self-Esteem and Narcissistic Injury

While Extreme Narcissists often *appear* to have high self-esteem, their grandiose self-image usually inflates their assets (or invents them whole cloth) and denies the reality of their deficits. In actual fact, the exaggerated self-esteem demonstrated by the Extreme Narcissist embodies a kind of lie; it reflects an ongoing effort of self-deception that is meant to deceive everyone else at the same time. Extreme Narcissists may sometimes appear indifferent to the opinions of other people, but in fact they always care deeply about how they are seen.

Because human beings are social animals, we develop our sense of self and self-worth within a social context, in relation to others. I may build self-respect by living up to my own standards and ideals, but I also need the important people in my life (my significant others, my colleagues and employers, my teachers) to respect me. If they do, that experience contributes to and supports my sense of self-worth. When they criticize me, even if I have a fairly robust sense of self, it may very well *hurt*. As a social animal, I naturally crave the approbation of the other members of my "pack," and to receive their disapproval instead would *wound* me, shaking my sense of self-worth . . . at least for a time.

In the language of my profession, these blows to one's self-esteem are referred to as *narcissistic injuries*. While psychoanalysts and psychologists usually discuss narcissistic injury in the context of mental disorders, it's actually a universal aspect of everyday life: On a regular basis (and more often than you might imagine), each of us must deal with challenges to our self-esteem in the form of disapproval, slights, and rejection.

Your English professor gives you a C on that paper you felt so good about.

Somebody else gets the job you thought you were perfect for.

After your first date (which you thought amazing), the other person won't return your calls.

On occasion, we all go through these types of experiences. If only for a brief time, they may challenge your sense of personal worth and make you question the view you hold of yourself.

Maybe I'm not as smart and insightful as I thought.

Maybe I'm not as highly skilled as I like to believe.

Maybe I'm not such a great catch after all.

You don't necessarily voice such doubts to yourself in exactly this way, but you will *feel* them. Your face might go hot with chagrin, the world might suddenly seem a darker and less hospitable place. You might feel humiliated or grow downcast and depressed. We have all felt this way at one time or another.

Narcissistic injuries are inevitable, and different people respond to them in a variety of ways. Individuals with especially low self-esteem may isolate themselves and withdraw from contact, unable to show their face. Others find ways to ward off the pain by invalidating the source of it.

Professor X has never liked me, not from day one.

I didn't get that job because I'm overqualified.

Now that I think about it, our date wasn't really all that special.

In essence, these defensive maneuvers are *lies* we tell ourselves to ward off the truth and shore up our self-esteem. Often, they're temporary measures that soften the blow, and we'll eventually face the truth once the pain has eased. Some people are unable to tolerate the smallest blow to their self-esteem and will never back down from defensiveness. As we shall see, Extreme Narcissists find such blows to their fragile sense of self-worth to be so unbearably painful that they are constantly on guard against them, *even before they occur.*

But we all must face these challenges to our self-esteem. They're inevitable.

To illustrate the everyday nature of narcissistic injury and our reactions to it, I'd like to describe one particularly awful day in the life of Natalie, a young woman in her midtwenties who works as a legal assistant at a midsized law firm in Atlanta.

"IT'S JUST NOT FAIR"

Natalie wakes up in a bad mood because she has once again slept through her alarm clock and is going to be late for work. She has a vague recollection of hitting the snooze button more than once . . . she probably should've gotten to bed earlier, instead of watching those two episodes of *Homeland* on Netflix. Natalie takes a quick shower, wolfs down a protein bar, and is about to leave the apartment when she spots a note from her roommate, Selena, on the kitchen counter. Selena is an assistant producer for one of the morning programs on CNN and usually starts work before dawn.

"Hey Natalie," the note reads. "Just a quick reminder that it was your turn to clean the bathroom this week." Natalie feels irritated by the row of smiley faces that Selena has placed above her signature. "Neat freak," she says aloud, on her way out the door.

Climbing into her car, Natalie recalls with a smile that she and Brian have a date scheduled for that night. They've been going out for only a couple of months, but she feels it's starting to get serious. Brian is an attractive guy with an offbeat sense of humor and a great job at Ernst & Young. They have a lot of interests in common. She has lately begun to wonder if he might turn out to be marriage material.

Because she didn't leave home early enough, Natalie has run into the worst of the commuter traffic on the interstate and arrives at work even later than usual. She always makes up the missed time at the end of the day (plus, her bosses, Dan and Matthew, usually roll in much later than she does), but she still feels bad that she can't get to work on time, despite repeated resolutions to do better. Nina, the receptionist, smiles and says, "Forty-five minutes—now that must be a record!" Feeling hot and irritable, Natalie shoots back, "There was an accident on I-75—it's not my fault!" Even though she knows this is a lie, she feels justified in her self-defense.

Settling down at the computer, she pulls up her calendar and notes that her annual performance review with Barbara, the head of personnel, is scheduled for eleven. She'd forgotten all about it. With so much work in her in-box, the morning passes quickly. Natalie is a little nervous about the impending performance review but mostly she's looking forward to a raise. She's been with the firm for two years now and hasn't had a raise since starting. Of course there have been some "glitches" in her work product—nobody's perfect—but all in all, she's done a pretty good job. She *deserves* a raise.

Barbara calls Natalie into her office at 11:00 on the dot. She's extremely punctual, almost to a fault, and a stickler for details. She gives Natalie one of those big phony smiles that are her trademark and launches into the review, handing a single sheet of paper across the desk so that Natalie will have her own copy of the evaluation.

As she runs her eyes down the column, Natalie sees a fairly straight line of number 3s—*Satisfactory*. She also *Needs Improvement* in a couple of areas: "Punctuality" and "Attention to Detail." Overall, her performance has received a 3, but there's a short minus sign after the number. Natalie feels the heat in her face and scalp; tears fill her eyes, and she fights them back. For one moment, she has the panicky urge to go running. She keeps her eyes downcast because she finds it hard, almost painful, to meet Barbara's gaze.

"The lateness isn't a major concern," Barbara says, "not in and of itself. As you know, we're fairly casual around here and we all appreciate that you're so careful to make up any time you miss." When Natalie looks up, Barbara is smiling at her with sympathy. The fact that she can sense Barbara trying to be gentle only makes her feel worse.

"We're more concerned about the number of unnecessary mistakes in your work product. Both Dan and Matthew feel you tend to rush through things. Maybe it's because you're so often late and playing catch-up, but we'd all like you to slow down and double-check your work from now on." A memory springs suddenly to mind: last week, the call from the messenger service down at court because she'd forgotten to include a check for the filing fee along with the Davis complaint. She'd come in late that day, too, and had felt frazzled all morning.

Back at her own desk, Natalie has a hard time focusing. Barbara's words from the performance review keep intruding into her thoughts, disrupting her concentration. She tries to remember whether she told Selena or Brian about the upcoming performance review. Maybe she won't have to say a word about it to either one of them. As the afternoon wears on, Natalie wonders whether she should start looking for a new job, a *better* job with a higher salary. Law firms are so stuffy, lawyers so boring. This hasn't turned out to be the exciting place she imagined when she started. Maybe Selena can help her get a job in television. She'd probably do better surrounded by more creative types.

Near quitting time, Natalie decides to cancel her date with Brian. Given her dark mood, she'd probably make poor company. She might start crying. If Brian were to ask her why, she couldn't avoid telling him about the performance review, and she's afraid he might think she's a "loser." Right now, all she wants is to go home, curl up in bed with a pint of Häagen Dazs, and watch the final few episodes of *Homeland*. She reaches for her cell phone and sees that Brian called earlier in the day, during her meeting with Barbara, and has left a message. Her heartbeat speeds up a little at the sound of his voice.

"Hey Natalie, it's me, Brian. Calling about tonight. Listen, I'm not going to be able to make it. Actually . . . God, I really don't want to do this over voicemail. Call me back when you can—we need to talk."

Hearing those four dreadful words, *we need to talk*, Natalie feels as if the bottom has dropped out of her world. The pain of the day has overwhelmed her. She stifles a small scream as her eyes well up with tears. When Nina, the receptionist, walks by, Natalie startles her by snarling, "Men are such assholes! It's just not fair!"

Like all of us, Natalie must cope with narcissistic injury as an inevitable part of life. This particular day may have proven especially painful, piling up the challenges to her self-esteem one after the other, but there's nothing unusual about the narcissistic injuries she experiences or the ways she reacts to them.

She begins her day feeling bad about herself because she hasn't yet found a way to wake up and get to work on time. On some level, she knows that her lateness is the result of poor choices she makes (deciding to watch *Homeland* instead of turning off the lights and going to sleep). Her roommate's reminder that she forgot to clean the bathroom only makes Natalie feel worse, but she deflects that feeling with a critical thought about Selena: "Neat freak." *It's not that I dropped the ball; the problem is that Selena is a perfectionist.* At work when the receptionist makes a crack about her lateness, Natalie takes similar evasive action: "It's not my fault!"

Shifting blame is one of the most common strategies for evading the pain of narcissistic injury.

Looking forward to a pay raise and expecting a positive evaluation, Natalie is devastated by her performance review. Tears come to her eyes; she feels hot and humiliated. While she had successfully warded off the earlier challenges to her self-esteem, she can't escape this time and feels trapped (at least for the moment). She knows that what Barbara has told her is true. As the day wears on, however, she begins to recover: She belittles the stuffy, boring nature of law firms and persuades herself she's a more creative type who'd do better in a different environment.

Taking refuge in superiority or expressing contempt for the source of a narcissistic injury is another common strategy for evading that pain.

Despite these efforts to shore up her self-esteem, Natalie's day has shaken her badly. She feels as if she's a "loser," though she attributes that thought to Brian (how he might view her if he knew about her poor performance review). Overwhelmed by her painful day, she wants to cancel their date and retreat to her bed-nest where she can comfort herself. When she hears the voice message and realizes that Brian intends to dump her, she feels shattered. She almost immediately wards off the pain, however, taking refuge in feelings of rage and indignation at the way in which women are treated in the dating world: "Men are such assholes!"

Angry indignation is a third common response to narcissistic injury, an attempt to evade pain by going on the attack.

Extreme Narcissists rely heavily on these three defensive maneuvers, as we shall see in later chapters. In constant need of support for their inflated self-image, they can't tolerate even the smallest criticism and may launch an aggressive attack against the person who faults or rejects them:

They will blame you for their own mistakes.

They will treat their detractors with superiority and contempt.

They may become enraged and respond indignantly to even the smallest challenge to their self-esteem.

Reacting defensively to criticism is an extremely common response, one might even say a *universal* human reaction. Dale Carnegie made this point long ago in his 1936 classic, *How to Win Friends and Influence People*, the original self-help book: "Criticism is futile because it puts a person on the defensive and usually makes him strive to justify himself. Criticism is dangerous, because it wounds a person's 'precious pride,' hurts his sense of importance, and arouses resentment."[1]

Criticism can be dangerous primarily because the person you have criticized often feels *attacked*, no matter how sensitively you try to phrase your comments, and she may retaliate in kind. Because you have wounded her "precious pride," she may feel as if you deliberately intended to hurt her, and then she'll try to hurt you back. Such counterattacks stem from a psychological tendency I refer to as the principle of false attribution: *I feel pain, and therefore someone must be responsible for causing me to feel that way.*

It's a very common experience, best illustrated by the occasional irritability we all experience from time to time when we're extremely tired and running low on emotional reserves. At such moments, it often seems that the people around us are behaving in *incredibly annoying ways*. The things they do, the questions they ask, the small "mistakes" they make seem to *explain or account for* the irritation we're feeling. As a result, we may snap or lash out at them, convinced they deserve such treatment for their irritating behavior, when, in fact, we're just being "grouchy." Such irritability is an uncomfortable, even painful state of mind; due to the principle of false attribution, we assume other people are the cause of our pain.

When Natalie reads Selena's gentle reminder note, it makes her feel badly about herself. On some level, she feels attacked, as if Selena *intended* her to feel badly (despite those smiley faces!) and mentally retaliates: *Neat freak.* The principle of false attribution helps us to understand the Extreme Narcissists in our world as well. You may not recognize what you've done to wound their pride, or you may feel baffled by violent reactions to seemingly innocent comments or actions that had nothing to do with them; but in some invisible way, they feel painfully diminished and therefore *under attack*.

In other words, the Extreme Narcissist experiences each narcissistic injury as an assault that stirs up pain, and he will retaliate, often violently, against the "cause" of it.

THE POWER OF SHAME

The term *narcissistic injury* sounds a bit abstract and technical, remote from our immediate feeling states. What emotion do we actually feel when our self-esteem is wounded? A narcissistic injury *hurts*, of course—for the Extreme Narcissist as well as the rest of us—but what is the exact nature of that pain? Looking back over Natalie's day, you'll see that in each instance, *shame and humiliation* lie at the heart of her pain.

Recognizing that she has made some poor decisions relating to her need for sleep, she feels mildly ashamed of herself. The note from Selena pointing out that Natalie forgot to clean the bathroom intensifies her shame. When the receptionist teases her about being especially late that day, she feels both ashamed and humiliated. The performance review stirs up more shame because she knows that Barbara is right—she *does* have a tendency to rush through her work and make careless mistakes; she feels humiliated by hearing the truth. When Brian makes it clear he intends to break off their relationship, she experiences his rejection as yet another humiliation. This awful day has inspired a deep and agonizing sense of shame about herself, as if she's a "loser."

In this light, defensive maneuvers for evading the pain of narcissistic injury (such as blaming, contempt, and indignation) are more accurately described as *defenses against shame*. Efforts to evade feelings of shame and humiliation play a central role in narcissism. In fact, as psychologist Andrew Morrison has noted, shame is the "underside of narcissism" and central to an understanding of it.[2] In the next chapter we'll take a closer look at the profound type of shame that can make one feel like a *total loser*, and the ways the Extreme Narcissist tries to prove that he's a winner instead.

As a psychotherapist, I work with defenses against shame on a daily basis. Many of my clients rely on what we might call *narcissistic defenses* to ward off feelings of shame or inferiority. Take my client Jason, who began his session one day complaining about his wife, Diana. Jason had promised to call their accountant earlier in the week to set up an appointment but then forgot all about it. The night before our session, Diana had complained that he was unreliable, that he "always" dropped the ball on his commitments. From there, the conversation escalated into a full-blown fight.

"I don't see why she had to make such a big deal about it," Jason told me. "I was superstressed at work all week and just forgot. Plus I hate the way she has to make it about what I 'always' do, like I'm this really bad person. I know I probably shouldn't have, but I slammed out and told her she was a bitch."

Jason went on at some length about his wife's critical, perfectionistic nature and her tendency to engage in character assassination during their arguments. As I listened, it struck me as one of those marital fights that actually concern *something else*, an emotional issue at work behind the scenes. Both Diana's reaction to the forgotten appointment and Jason's defensive response seemed overly intense and out of proportion to the actual event. This particular interaction had a back history, of course—the other promises Jason hadn't kept, Diana's tendency to be overly critical—but that didn't seem to account for the emotional heat. By that point, I knew Jason fairly well and I wondered aloud whether his wife might be complaining about some *other* way in which he was letting her down. His defensiveness suggested that he didn't want to admit she might have a right to complain.

As the session evolved, it seemed likely that the actual focus of Diana's disappointment was their sex life, or lack thereof. Earlier in the week, she had tried to initiate sex and he'd once again turned her down, relying on the usual excuse of fatigue and work-related stress. When Jason told me about his wife's angry complaint that they so rarely had intercourse, his entire manner and tone of voice had changed. No longer defensive, he seemed awash in shame. I asked whether the lack of sex might have to do with his long-standing involvement with Internet pornography; he finally acknowledged what he hadn't wanted to admit, not even to me, his therapist: that he'd lately been watching porn and masturbating on a daily basis. He knew he ought to stop, that it was bad for his marriage, but no matter how hard he tried, he always went back.

Jason is not an Extreme Narcissist, but he relies on *narcissistic defenses* to cope with his shame. Like Natalie, who feels shame because she's unable to change her behavior and get to work on time, Jason is ashamed of his uncontrollable addiction to pornography, so much so that he doesn't even want to mention it during his own session. Instead, he focuses on a comparatively trivial fight during which he became *indignant* (slamming the door) and *shifted blame* onto his wife (faulting her for being critical). He even takes refuge in *superiority and contempt* (calling her a bitch), all in order to ward off the shame he feels about his addiction to pornography. (We'll discuss more about the relationship between shame, addiction, and narcissism in Chapter Ten.)

Like Jason, Extreme Narcissists often hurt those around them as they try to shore up their sense of self. No doubt Diana felt frustrated and lonely, but also wounded when Jason called her a bitch; the Extreme Narcissist causes a similar but more intense type of pain to the people they know, sometimes taking direct action to inflict a wound rather than merely using hurtful words. You might have been on the receiving end of such behavior—on the job, in your family, or with a member of your social set. You may find much in common with Lizzie, who nearly lost her job because of a broken friendship.

"YOU DON'T SEE IT AT FIRST"

When Lizzie's cat died, Denise left a condolence card on her desk at work, along with a bud vase holding a single rose from her garden. Denise had started at Carlyle & Co. only a month before, so the two women didn't know each other well. A few weeks later, Denise invited Lizzie out to lunch and they hit it off immediately. They enjoyed the same kind of music, liked the same TV shows, and had a passion for classic film noir. They both thought that Ryan Gosling was the sexiest actor in Hollywood. Denise told Lizzie she had great taste in clothes and she laughed at all her jokes, which was gratifying because it often seemed to Lizzie that people didn't understand her quirky sense of humor. It felt so good to have a new friend who really "got" her.

They started spending a lot of time together outside of the office—drinks after work, dinner on weekends, movie nights when they'd make popcorn and watch an old favorite, like Bogart and Bacall in *The Big Sleep*. Not a day went by without a phone call, many text messages, and a chain of emails going back and forth. Denise often told Lizzie she was "an amazing person" and how lucky she, Denise, felt to have her as a friend. Now and then, Lizzie suggested they ask someone else from work to join them for drinks and appetizers at their favorite bar; Denise would make a face and say "Maybe another time."

Lizzie invited Denise to join a group of her other friends at a dance club one Saturday night. It seemed to go well, but then at lunch on Monday, Denise dropped a few snide remarks about Cady ("Somebody ought to tell her not to go bare-midriffed, not with those muffin tops") and Steph ("That laugh! She sounds like a deranged hyena"). Lizzie thought Denise might be jealous of her other friendships; maybe it would pass as they all got to know one another and Denise felt more included.

When Denise invited her to have lunch later that week, Lizzie told her she'd already made plans: An old friend from high school happened to be in town for a few days and this would be their one chance to catch up. Afterward, when they ran into one another in the corridor, Denise seemed distant and chilly. But within a few days, she warmed up and their friendship seemed to go back to normal. That weekend, they went to see the new Ryan Gosling movie.

Then Lizzie met Mark. She couldn't wait to tell Denise all about it—how they both reached for the same bottle of wine, the last one on the shelf at the wine shop, leading to a flirtatious tussle over possession, full of innuendo. Mark finally said he'd let Lizzie claim the wine if she'd give him her telephone number.

"I'm so happy for you!" Denise said. Her smile seemed forced;

her voice cracked on a high note of enthusiasm. "Just be careful. You know how guys are. Lots of them are jerks but you don't see it at first."

Lizzie felt a little annoyed by Denise's response but shrugged it off. Later that week, when Denise suggested they get together on Saturday, Lizzie told her she already had a date with Mark. Denise's eyes filled with tears. "I hope you're not one of those women who drop their friends just because a new guy comes along. You're my best friend—don't you know how much you mean to me?" Lizzie felt guilty and tried to mollify her by suggesting they get together on Sunday. All of a sudden, Denise turned angry, brushing away her tears. "I'm busy," she said, and she stormed off in a huff.

From the moment Lizzie and Mark arrived at the restaurant on Saturday night, Denise began texting questions. *What's he wearing? What kind of car does he drive?* Lizzie answered, *I'll tell you all about it later* and turned off her phone. When she turned it back on at the end of the evening, after Mark had dropped her off at her apartment, she found a long stream of increasingly angry texts—about what a bad friend she was, what a two-faced, selfish bitch—with one final curt message delivered after midnight: *Fuck you!!!* Although Lizzie had seen a few warning signs, the depth of this hostility stunned her. What had happened to the wonderful new friend who had always seemed so supportive?

At work on Monday, Denise stopped by Lizzie's office to apologize. She might have had a little too much to drink, she said, and lost control of her temper. "I'm really sorry. I know I've been a very bad girl, but can you forgive me?" Still upset by those vicious text messages, Lizzie didn't feel able to resume their friendship on the same terms as before. She didn't trust the puppy-dog smile Denise gave her.

"I need a break," she said. "Maybe it's better if we don't spend so much time together, at least for a while."

Denise's demeanor instantly changed. "Fine," she snarled, her voice full of contempt, "if that's the way you want to play it. I always knew you were a total phony." After Denise had stormed off, Lizzie felt so upset she couldn't stop shaking. Something about those final words had felt so ominous. The new friend who had seemed such a blessing now felt dangerous.

For the rest of the week, Lizzie steered clear of Denise. She didn't want any more ugly confrontations. Perhaps they'd drift apart now and their intense friendship would simply fade into the past. When Mark called to ask her out again for the coming weekend, her excitement about this new relationship eclipsed her worries.

The following day at work, one of her co-workers who'd known Lizzie for years approached her in the rest room and said Denise was talking trash about her. She had decided to break off their friendship (Denise was saying) because Lizzie had bailed in midevening too many times, ditching her whenever some random guy offered to buy her a drink. Another colleague told her that Denise hadn't exactly come out and said so but insinuated that Lizzie was a promiscuous drunk who went home with a different guy every night. Lizzie was in tears most of that day. She felt too afraid of Denise to confront her.

Meanwhile, Denise peppered her with abusive texts, all variations on a theme: *I was a good friend and you treated me like shit, you fucking bitch.* In one of her more bizarre texts, she complained of having *wasted the treasure of my regard and intimacy on a heartless guttersnipe.* Lizzie felt sure it was a line from some old movie but couldn't place it.

On Wednesday, the head of her department called Lizzie into his office, concerned over reports that she'd been dating one of the firm's clients—strictly against policy and grounds for dismissal. No doubt Denise had been the source of that rumor, too. Lizzie broke down sobbing and told her department head the whole story. When she showed him the string of abusive text messages from Denise on her phone, then brought in the co-worker who'd warned her about the other vicious rumors, he finally believed her. Carlyle & Co. dismissed Denise immediately, giving her a month's severance pay and a strong letter of recommendation. After witnessing her vindictive behavior, the boss didn't want to antagonize her and find the company on the end of a wrongful dismissal lawsuit.

When Denise continued sending her abusive text messages, Lizzie finally changed her cell number. She never saw Denise again.

Denise doesn't fit the profile for Narcissistic Personality Disorder, though she seems fairly disturbed. The way she alternates between idealizing and hating Lizzie, along with her explosive anger, fear of abandonment, and "affective instability," make her seem closer to Borderline Personality Disorder. At the same time, she seems quite narcissistic, with an inflated self-image and an inability to empathize. While not overtly grandiose, she needs to feel that she's the center of her best friend's universe. At the beginning of their friendship, she appears sensitive and considerate, but only because she wants to win Lizzie's affection. Once Lizzie rejects her, it becomes obvious that Denise has virtually no ability to empathize.

Although Denise may seem like an extreme case, visitors to my website, responding to a post I wrote about vindictive narcissism, have described even worse instances of abuse by former friends, co-workers, and relatives. More than one person described relentless campaigns by an ex-friend to destroy their reputation or drive them from the workplace. One man told how his narcissistic brother, a lawyer, was threatening to destroy his career and ruin him financially by abusing the legal system, all to cheat him out of his share of their parents' estate. One woman wrote about a former friend who tried to run her down with her truck in a parking lot.

The most harrowing accounts came from men and women who had been married to an Extreme Narcissist and found themselves persecuted and often terrorized following divorce. Like Denise, who felt rejection as a kind of narcissistic injury and immediately struck back, the Extreme Narcissist finds divorce unbearably humiliating, an assault upon his or her self-image, and will often seek to persecute the former spouse with vicious zeal. We'll hear more about this type of Vindictive Narcissist in Chapter Nine.

These people don't always fit the profile for Narcissistic Personality Disorder. Like Denise, they may seem closer to Borderline Personality Disorder. Some of them come across as sociopaths. As explained in Chapter One, narcissism occurs along a continuum of possible expressions, especially within the other personality disorders but also in mania, paranoia, and bipolar disorder. Many people who don't fit any particular diagnosis may nonetheless become vengeful in similar if less dramatic ways when you offend them:

Your sister-in-law, angrily complaining to relatives about your supposedly harsh and critical nature, misrepresenting what you actually said, all because you questioned her judgment.

A friend of a friend, who starts bad-mouthing you when you didn't invite him to your party.

A colleague at work who seems to have it out for you, for no reason you can identify.

Sometimes you can guess what you might have done to stir up resentment, even if you believe the other person misunderstood you or is overreacting. Often, the source of the hatred is invisible.

Take a closer look and you'll notice that the overt behavior of these men and women seems to embody the type of narcissistic defenses I've been discussing in this chapter. When Lizzie starts dating Mark, Denise feels rejected and *blames* her for being a bad friend who "abandoned" her. She later becomes scornful and full of *contempt*, calling Lizzie a two-faced bitch and a phony. *Indignant rage*, fueling a vengeful urge to lash out and inflict harm, characterizes most of what she does as the friendship falls apart. It seems likely that Denise experiences Lizzie's rejection as a major narcissistic injury, stirring up a shameful sense of inferiority, even if we can't see the shame at work, as we do with Jason and Natalie.

Because their shame is so much deeper and more agonizing, Extreme Narcissists will stop at nothing to avoid feeling it. In fact, almost everything they say and do is intended to avoid the experience of shame. The narcissistic defenses they mobilize against shame are so extreme and pervasive that they color everything about the person's personality, relationships, and behavior, creating a kind of shell or armor against the threat of shame.

They may appear arrogant or haughty, as if to say *No shame here*. They try hard to come across as winners and prove that somebody else, quite possibly you, is the shame-ridden loser. Instead of acknowledging the unconscious shame they feel, as well as their envy for other successful people with high self-esteem, they persuade themselves that it is actually those others who feel the envy. And when faced with narcissistic injury, their response is typically swift, brutal, and ruthless as they seek to annihilate shame and the external source of it. As one visitor to my site commented, there is something almost *reptilian* in the way an Extreme Narcissist will reflexively strike out when confronted with a threat to his self-esteem. They sometimes seem cold-blooded, almost inhuman.

In summary, the personality and behavior of Extreme Narcissists disguise the unconscious shame they can't bear to feel, concealing it from themselves and from the rest of the world. For this reason, we may at first find it almost impossible to understand what drives them and can only *infer* it from certain behaviors or character traits. The following checklist will help you to identify those features in people you know and perhaps determine whether the especially difficult person in your life might be an Extreme Narcissist.

Unlike the DSM, which requires that a person demonstrate a minimum number of features to qualify for a diagnosis, the checklist below has no rigid requirements and isn't intended as a diagnostic tool. Rather, my goal is to help you recognize narcissistic traits in the people you know; all of the behaviors and characteristics listed below feature in Extreme Narcissism. The more of them that apply to someone you know, the more narcissistic that person.

I've grouped these traits into five categories that should help you focus on specific areas of concern. If you put a check mark next to more than one item in several groups, you're probably dealing with an Extreme Narcissist. If many of the items in most of the categories seem to apply, the person likely meets the diagnostic criteria for Narcissistic Personality Disorder.

"I'm Easily Wounded": Self-Esteem and Narcissistic Injury

A. <u>Empathy and Emotions</u>

_____Feels uncomfortable with his or her emotional life

_____Lacks interest in you and your feelings

_____Criticizes you for feeling "too much" or for "overreacting"

_____When angry or upset, often denies feeling that way

_____Feels envious or imagines other people to be envious of him or her

_____Goes on the attack when hurt or frustrated; explodes with rage

_____Lacks insight into the way his or her behavior affects others

B. <u>Self-Image and Social Comparison</u>

_____Preoccupied with the way he or she is viewed by others

_____Arrogant, vain, and haughty; exaggerates accomplishments

_____Makes obvious plays for attention or admiration

_____Hypercompetitive and ambitious

_____Easily slighted; tends to misinterpret innocent remarks as put-downs

_____Makes contemptuous remarks about other people behind their backs

_____Ridicules you and makes you feel bad about yourself

C. <u>Impulsivity</u>

_____Lacks self-control; spends beyond his or her means

_____Overeats, drinks too much, or abuses drugs

_____Tends to be a workaholic

_____Initiates grand projects but can't follow through

_____Falls quickly in and out of idealized romantic love

_____Makes important life decisions with little forethought

_____Is unfaithful in marriage or committed relationships

D. Interpersonal Relationships

_____Is self-absorbed, controlling, and exploitative

_____Can be seductive and manipulative

_____Tends to be overly jealous and possessive

_____Dominates conversation and frequently interrupts others

_____Is suspicious of other people's motives, always imagining the worst

_____Demands uncritical allegiance

_____Bullies others to get his or her way

E. Moral Code and Personal Responsibility

_____Lies or distorts the truth for personal gain

_____Blames others or makes excuses for his or her mistakes

_____Plays the victim; uses guilt to manipulate you

_____Engages in illegal or unethical behavior

_____Feels entitled to have what he or she wants

_____Comes across as self-righteous and bulletproof during arguments

_____Inspires self-doubt when you disagree; shames or humiliates you

If we were to evaluate Denise according to this checklist, or Naomi from Chapter One, we'd probably put marks next to a couple of statements from Groups A, B, D, and E. They're Extreme Narcissists who don't meet the full criteria for Narcissistic Personality

Disorder—unlike Sam, who would earn several check marks in all five groups. And because narcissism occurs along a continuum, bear in mind that most of us could be described by at least a few of these statements.

It's all a question of degree.

"I'M A WINNER AND YOU'RE A LOSER"
The Bullying Narcissist

It should come as no surprise that many Extreme Narcissists are highly competitive in virtually every area of their lives, whether in athletics, the business world, or the social milieu they inhabit. They *need* to win at sports, destroy the competition in their given field, or feel that they are wealthier, more popular, better looking, or more admired than other people—that is, the social "winners" in their world. Whatever the domain, victory in competition supports their inflated sense of self: they are the winners who prove themselves superior to the losers they defeat. And they need to go on proving it, again and again.

For Extreme Narcissists, there are only two classes of people: those who are on top and those who are below. They typically "divide the world into famous, rich, and great people on the one hand, and the despicable, worthless 'mediocrity' on the other." They are afraid of not belonging to the former group and "belonging instead to the 'mediocre,' by which they mean worthless and despicable rather than 'average' in the ordinary sense of the term."[1] This division of the world into two classes of people, the *winners* and the *losers*, defines the narcissistic worldview, and for this reason, these words will come up again and again in our discussion.

Just as a comedian might rely on a straight man to make himself seem funny, the Extreme Narcissist exploits the loser as a kind of foil to his winner self-image. Through his arrogance and haughty manner—*I'm better than you*—he forces the other person into a supporting role as his inferior. And although it might not be obvious, he *needs* that other person: When it comes to competition, somebody else must lose in order for him to become the winner. In short, the Extreme Narcissist boosts his self-image at the other person's expense.

Many Extreme Narcissists are also bullies who compete in the social realm and make their victims feel like social losers. This behavior usually comes to the fore in middle school, when children emerge from the relative safety of their neighborhood elementary school into a much larger world in which nearly everyone is insecure about his or her social status. Bullies search out losers over whom they can triumph, relying on physical and emotional intimidation to promote their own standing at the expense of their victims.

"I'M NOT THE LOSER—YOU ARE"

Bullies have always been around, of course, but the arrival of the Internet and the explosion of social media platforms have given them a new arena in which to act. In recent years, the phenomenon of cyberbullying has made headlines. To take one of many examples: On September 9, 2013, national papers and TV news programs broke the story of twelve-year-old Rebecca Sedwick, who committed suicide by throwing herself from a tower located in an abandoned cement plant in Florida. For months prior to her death, Sedwick had been subjected to a cyberbullying campaign allegedly spearheaded by Guadalupe Shaw, a fourteen-year-old girl who used her popularity to mobilize a team of girls in the assault, persecuting other middle-school kids as well if they befriended Sedwick. Using text messages, Facebook, and a variety of social media platforms, Shaw told Sedwick she was ugly, that she should "drink bleach and die," and urged her to kill herself.

Shaw also allegedly persuaded another girl, Katelyn Roman, to beat up Rebecca Sedwick. Roman had once been Sedwick's best friend, and she eventually apologized for having bullied her. By contrast, Shaw expressed no remorse. According to the local sheriff in Florida, she appeared cold and emotionless upon her arrest. On her Facebook page, she acknowledged having bullied Sedwick and announced that she didn't "give a fuck" that her victim was dead. Shaw's parents allege their daughter never made that statement. They claim her Facebook account was hacked.

Not long after, in a strange twist to this unhappy story, Shaw's stepmother, Vivian Vosburg, was charged with two counts of child abuse and four counts of child neglect when a Facebook video surfaced that showed her repeatedly punching a boy with her fists while several girls in the same room laughed. At a press conference during which he played a part of the video, the local sheriff said it showed that such violence appeared "to be a normal way of life" in the household.

Vosburg was not married to Shaw's father, José Ramirez. The two had lived together for some time with her four children and his three, all between the ages of nine and fourteen. The several different surnames (implying multiple failed relationships or marriages) and a history of household violence describe a world so remote from "normal family life" that Guadalupe Shaw's alleged brutal, callous behavior doesn't come as a complete surprise. When you explore the background of the Bullying Narcissist, you often find a similar history of broken families, emotional chaos, and child abuse.

According to ego psychology, children who are victims of such abuse will often resort to "identification with the aggressor" in order to escape from pain and feelings of helplessness.[2] In other words, instead of feeling victimized, they will victimize others: *I'm not the victim—you are.* We might also say that such children get rid of their painful feelings by off-loading (or projecting) them into other people. *I'm not the one who feels scared, helpless, and in pain—you are.*

I don't mean to suggest that all Extreme Narcissists were abused as children, though many of them come from turbulent, dysfunctional families where physical and emotional violence were routine. This early experience has a defining, pervasive influence: Because we need empathic, well-attuned parents in order to build healthy self-esteem, children born into chaos may never feel good about themselves. At base, they may come to feel that they are "damaged goods" and will then spend a lifetime in flight from this painful sense of self. This dynamic lies at the heart of narcissism.

The personality and behavior of the Extreme Narcissist embody a relentless effort to escape from feelings of defectiveness and inferiority. Despite appearances to the contrary, narcissism is the opposite of healthy self-esteem.

The projection of unwanted or unbearable experience into a "carrier" explains a great deal about the relationship between the Bullying Narcissist and her victim. The bully off-loads her painful sense of herself as damaged goods and forces the victim to feel it instead. *I'm not the loser—you are.* Projection, like all defense mechanisms, occurs unconsciously, outside of awareness: That is, bullies don't knowingly and intentionally try to off-load their painful sense of self, though their behavior reveals the unconscious process at work. By persecuting other people and making them feel like losers, the bully gets rid of her own loser self and persuades herself she's actually a winner.

Because the victims serve as carriers, their emotional experience helps us to understand how Bullying Narcissists actually (that is, unconsciously) feel themselves. The bully rarely comes for psychotherapy unless legally compelled to do so, but over the years, I've worked with several men who were the victims of bullying in their youth. One of them, Ryan, bore the scars for life. As a tween, he was bullied by a group of kids in middle school, both boys and girls, and in particular by Danny, another player on his soccer team. The history of Ryan and Danny's relationship shows how the bully can "force" a victim to carry his projected sense of shame.

A BROKEN "BLUEPRINT FOR NORMALITY"

Ryan's father worked in the oil and gas industry and had spent many years living in Asia. When he returned to the United States to take a job in his native Colorado, he brought with him a Taiwanese wife and their infant son, Ryan. The father's new employer was located in a small city whose population was largely Caucasian, with some Hispanics and very few people of Asian descent, its economy dominated by military installations and the national headquarters of a conservative religious foundation. Within a few years, another son was born—Ryan's brother, Hunter.

When Ryan began therapy twenty-five years later, he described his early childhood as unremarkable, with no major family traumas. His father was a timid, disengaged figure eclipsed and dominated by Ryan's mother, a formidable woman who clearly viewed her husband as a failure and treated him with blatant contempt. She was also prodigiously ambitious and had founded a property management firm not long after her arrival in the United States, growing it into a highly successful enterprise. Along with her two sisters who still lived in Taiwan, she also ran an import-export business. Preoccupied with her business ventures, she took little emotional interest in her sons, though she directed and controlled virtually all aspects of their lives.

Even during elementary school, Ryan felt somehow different from his peers, and not merely because of the way he looked, with his mother's complexion and almond-shaped eyes. Shy and soft-spoken, with few friends, he saw himself as lacking some essential quality, the confidence and vitality he could identify in many of the other boys. His mother signed him up for the soccer league and insisted he continue playing, year after year, though he didn't enjoy the sport. When it was his mother's turn to provide snacks for a match, Ryan felt embarrassed by the Taiwanese treats she sent along—pineapple cake and *gua-bao*, rather than the prepackaged treats brought by the American mothers.

Ryan was twelve years old and had entered middle school when his brother, Hunter, was formally diagnosed with Asperger's syndrome, and the teasing began. Hunter had always seemed peculiar, with his strangely formal speech and refusal to use contractions, the odd bouncing way he walked, on the balls of his feet and leaning forward. Some of the boys in middle school would taunt Ryan about his brother the "freak." Or they would mimic Hunter's speech in

Ryan's presence, emphatically pronouncing the words *will not* instead of *won't*, or *cannot* instead of *can't*. Later, the teasing focused on the shape of Ryan's eyes. Even the other boys on his soccer team, teammates for several years, began to mock him. Danny, the captain of the team, became head bully and relentlessly persecuted Ryan.

Prior to adolescence, Danny had been a small and physically uncoordinated boy. Though his parents had divorced many years earlier, when Danny was only two, they continued feuding, publicly and through the court system. Ryan recalled one soccer match where Danny's parents both showed up (they usually took turns) and humiliated Danny by screaming at one another on the sidelines. Early on, Ryan had felt a kind of distant kinship with Danny because they both seemed like outsiders, different from the other "normal" kids. Middle school changed everything.

Over the summer before seventh grade, Danny shot up several inches and put on muscle. His looks improved. In the major reshuffling of social status that is middle school, he became one of the "cool" kids, highly popular with both boys and girls. When Danny mocked Ryan in the hallway, calling him a "gook," other kids followed his example. When Danny told friends he thought Ryan must be gay, the rumor quickly spread. Boys began shoving Ryan into his locker as they passed. Groups of girls would point and snicker from adjoining tables in the cafeteria. At soccer practice, his teammates would deliberately trip him up and laugh when he fell.

Over his mother's objections, Ryan quit soccer. When he finally told her about the bullying, she shrugged and told him he needed to get tough. He felt that she viewed him with contempt—as a weakling, like his father. Ryan knew better than to ask for help from his dad, who seemed increasingly remote from the rest of the family. Over the next two years, as the bullying continued, Ryan's shame and sense of humiliation became so acute that he considered killing himself. He wished he were invisible; most of the time, he shunned involvement with other kids.

With yet another change of social landscape in high school, Ryan suddenly found he was no longer a target, though the legacy of shame and humiliation haunted him throughout his teens and into adulthood. Late in his twenties, Ryan finally sought professional help, afflicted with self-hatred so profound he felt almost crippled by it. Not long before we began working together, he'd taken a job with a marketing firm, part of a team whose dominant male players were outgoing, boisterous, and self-confident—"overgrown frat boys," he called them—who joked and ribbed one another throughout the workday. Ryan felt he ought to be more like them and despised himself for being meek. Whenever one of his co-workers teased him for being so quiet, it revived the trauma of middle school, filling him with shame and self-loathing.

As a rule, the young Bullying Narcissist doesn't choose a victim with high self-esteem. He targets someone vulnerable, like Ryan—someone insecure and feeling somewhat out of place, already concerned that he may be a loser. The Bullying Narcissist resonates with his victim because, on an unconscious level, they both struggle with the same emotional issues. Before middle school, Ryan felt that he and Danny had something in common, both of them outsiders marked by their difference from the other "normal" kids.

Rebecca Sedwick, the Florida girl who committed suicide, was reared in a disturbing environment not unlike the one in which

Guadalupe Shaw had grown up. Without a bed of her own, Sedwick slept on a recliner in the living room of their apartment and kept her clothes in paper grocery bags. Her mother, Tricia Norman, operated under several different aliases and had repeatedly tangled with the law for writing bad checks. The father took no part in family life.

Since the Bullying Narcissist unconsciously seeks to off-load his sense of defect or inferiority onto a carrier, it makes sense that he will choose someone primed to carry it—not a high-status peer but a person from a troubled background already struggling with low self-esteem. Though Ryan came from an intact family, his father was withdrawn and passive, his dominant mother controlling, contemptuous, and emotionally disengaged. His brother suffered from Asperger's syndrome. If bullies often come from troubled backgrounds, so do their victims.

According to British psychoanalyst D. W. Winnicott, humans are born into this world with an innate "blueprint for normality," a set of built-in expectations for how caretakers will respond to our physical and emotional needs.[3] In order to help us grow and feel good about ourselves, parents don't have to be perfect, just "good enough" in Winnicott's words. They need to be fairly well attuned to our needs and able to empathize closely with our emotional experience. Through their praise and attention, parents make us feel that we are understood, admired, and loved, thus laying the foundation for our healthy self-esteem.

When the environment diverges dramatically from that blueprint for normality, when parents are negligent and/or can't empathize, the growing child senses that something is *very wrong* in her world. On a deep intuitive level, she knows that her own development has gone awry; as a result, she may come to feel that she is deformed or ugly, inferior to other people. I refer to the excruciating sense of internal defect or ugliness as *core shame* because it afflicts a person at her core, coloring everything about her personality, behavior, and worldview.

My use of the word *shame* to describe this painful state may seem unfamiliar. Due to the work of popular psychology writers like John Bradshaw, most people have come to think of shame as the result of toxic, largely verbal messages from parents and other significant people in the growing child's world, something imposed from the outside.[4] By contrast, core shame takes hold in the earliest months of life, before language has developed; it is rooted in failed attachment relationships between mother and child and thrives in a chaotic atmosphere like the one Guadalupe Shaw experienced, one marred by violence or trauma.

This type of shame is felt as a profound, often unconscious sense of defect or inner ugliness. Children afflicted by core shame often feel that they are "damaged goods" or losers, an experience so excruciating and unbearable that they rely on various psychological defense mechanisms to deny or get rid of the pain. As described above, they often off-load (or project) their shame into someone else and make the other person feel it instead.

I'm not suggesting that a conscious decision is made to off-load shame, and, in reality, it's not actually possible to rid oneself of an unwanted feeling by forcing it on somebody else. Psychological defenses are largely unconscious "lies" we tell ourselves to evade pain, fantasies that are not bound by the laws of reality. On an unconscious level, I may deceive myself and come to believe that the shame is no longer my own but yours instead. As a result, I may consciously feel certain that *you* are the defective, ugly, shame-ridden loser, not me.

I may take aggressive action to prove it. In particular, I will feel driven to bolster my image as a winner, superior to the shame-ridden losers I defeat.

The pursuit of a "winner" image as a defense against core shame, rooted in the earliest years of life, lies at the heart of Extreme Narcissism.

The Lance Armstrong saga—his relentless pursuit of winning at all costs, the heroic image he cultivated, and the brutal way he bullied his detractors—offers a dramatic, well-publicized illustration of this dynamic. While we can't access Armstrong's inner life, so much of what has come to light about his past is suggestive. Like Guadalupe Shaw, he is the product of a world that diverged dramatically from Winnicott's blueprint for normality.

WINNING AT ANY COST

Armstrong's mother, Linda, had grown up in the Dallas projects, living in a series of grim tenements that "smelled like cat box" and reeked of "the anger and brokenness of previous tenants."[5] Her alcoholic father physically abused her mother, then abandoned her . . . though he still showed up at her door for years afterward, spending the night and leaving her with a few new bruises by which to remember him. The Armstrong saga begins in a world of broken marriages and emotional violence.

Linda was a junior in high school when she became pregnant by her boyfriend Edward ("Eddie") Gunderson. Eddie reluctantly agreed to marry Linda, but even before the birth of their child, it was clear that he was "chafing under the pressure of impending fatherhood." He began to leave bruises on her arms and neck where he had grabbed her, shoving her up against the wall when she scolded about the money he had spent or if she begged him not to go out drinking again with his buddies.

Their son, Lance Edward Gunderson, was born on September 18, 1971, when Linda was seventeen years old. The overwhelmed new parents fought constantly. Within a few months, Linda had moved into her father's apartment, where she and her baby slept on the couch. For months afterward, Eddie followed Linda to work, harassing her and insisting they move back in together. When she refused, he poured sugar into her gas tank and slashed the tires on her car. After two years of legal battles mediated by police and the court system, Linda successfully banished Eddie from her life. He never saw his child again.

A year or so after the divorce decree, Linda married Terry Keith Armstrong, a traveling salesman. Though Lance took his stepfather's last name, the two never bonded. According to Linda, she and Lance lived a more or less independent existence, due to the fact that Terry was usually on the road Monday through Friday. On the weekends, Terry regularly used to "paddle" the boy. A hypercompetitive man himself, Terry did take an interest in Lance's career as a young triathlete but ridiculed the boy if he cried, imposing his strict, traditional ideas of manhood upon him.[6] The older Lance grew, the more he and his stepfather clashed, eventually coming to physical blows. When Linda and Terry finally divorced after ten years of marriage, the teenage Lance threw a party.

The respective family backgrounds of Guadalupe Shaw, Rebecca Sedwick, and Lance Armstrong have much in common: multiple failed marriages, extreme poverty, an atmosphere of physical and emotional violence. For these three children, childhood deviated dramatically from the "blueprint for normality" Winnicott describes, and it is under these conditions that core shame takes root. Guadalupe Shaw seems to have dealt with her own shame by inflicting it upon her victim, boosting her own status as a winner by humiliating and persecuting Rebecca Sedwick, the loser.

Lance Armstrong's relentless bullying of those who challenged his heroic self-image points to a similar dynamic. Despite its many lies and misrepresentations, Armstrong's first book, *It's Not about the Bike*, sheds light on the origins of his drive to become a winner.[7] "I had started with nothing," he tells us. "My mother was a secretary in Plano, Texas, but on my bike, I had become something. When other kids were swimming at the country club, I was biking for miles after school, because it was my chance."

Armstrong exaggerates the rags-to-riches aspect of his story to elicit our admiration, but this passage nonetheless tells us something important. Victory in competition, proving himself a winner instead of a loser, provided him with a means to escape from something unbearable. Follow the train of thought, and you'll see it's about *feeling as if you're nothing* rather than *having* nothing. He may have felt like a loser, inferior to those kids at the country club with their stable, intact family lives; but on his bike he became a winner.

According to his two autobiographical books, Armstrong approached virtually every area of his life as a competition in which he could prove himself a winner. He describes a world full of adversaries over whom he has triumphed, one after the other, inviting us to admire his combative spirit. When diagnosed with cancer in 1996, he viewed the disease as his enemy, too. "I was not a compliant cancer patient. I was salty, aggressive, and pestering. I personalized the disease. 'The Bastard,' I called it. I made it my enemy, my challenge."

A determination to "beat" cancer is common among those afflicted by the disease, but Armstrong raised the battle to a new competitive level; he would eventually emerge the victor and cancer the *loser*.

This triumph over cancer and his subsequent first-place finish at the Tour de France made Armstrong a hero to millions, an all-around winner in every sense of the word, and a revered role model. Over the years, Armstrong repeatedly denied using illegal performance-enhancing drugs to earn all those gold medals. Such a world-class winner, a heroic athlete endowed with apparently superhuman strength and fortitude, didn't need to cheat.

When journalist David Walsh began to question the Armstrong myth, tracking down witnesses with knowledge of his program of illegal doping, Armstrong dubbed him the "little troll" and accused Walsh of conducting a "vendetta" against him. Though libel laws in the United States protected Walsh, Armstrong brought suit against him in the United Kingdom and other countries for defamation of character, negotiating a large out-of-court settlement with Walsh's newspaper, the *Sunday Times*, along with a public apology in print. Armstrong used his wealth, popularity, and his access to the media in order to bully Walsh into silence.

He also filed suit against one of Walsh's primary sources: Emma O'Reilly, former soigneur to the Armstrong team with personal knowledge of his illegal doping. On television and in public statements to the press, he assailed her character, referring to her as an alcoholic and a prostitute. When Betsy Andreu, the wife of a former teammate, also cooperated with Walsh, Armstrong likewise used his public stature to launch a counterattack, calling her a liar and a crazy bitch. No word describes this behavior better than *bullying*: Armstrong made use of his popularity and public stature to paint both women as losers.

"I'm a Winner and You're a Loser": The Bullying Narcissist

When the United States Anti-Doping Agency brought suit against him, Armstrong also called it a "vendetta" and launched his own retaliatory war in the press to discredit the doping agency and its charges. When former friends and teammates Greg LeMond, Floyd Landis, and Frankie Andreu publicly accused him of using illegal PEDs, he hired lawyers and launched a legal war to bully, silence, and defeat them. When he ran into former teammate Tyler Hamilton at a restaurant in Aspen, Armstrong became enraged, and allegedly threatened to make Hamilton's life a "living fucking hell" for having testified against him in the USADA suit.

Whatever his adversary's name, Armstrong was actually battling to protect his image as a winner. The fact that he had cheated to achieve his victories was irrelevant; the truth did not matter as long as the public perceived him as victorious. One of the stranger moments in the long Armstrong saga, in light of what we subsequently learned, was his public statement following his seventh Tour victory: "For the people that don't believe in cycling, the cynics and the skeptics, I'm sorry for you, I'm sorry you can't dream big. And I'm sorry you don't believe in miracles." He sounds utterly convincing, triumphant in his victory and contemptuous of his detractors, those losers who can't dream big.

Of course, it didn't matter that Win No. 7 was in fact no miracle but, rather, a chemically enhanced performance compliments of Dr. Michele Ferrari, the Italian mastermind behind Armstrong's doping program. For Armstrong, to lose in competition—to appear as a loser in the public's eye—represents the worst possible fate. He feels nothing but contempt for losers and has done everything he could—lying and cheating his way onto the winner's podium—to make sure he was never perceived as one of them. And through his access to the

press as well as the courts, he bullied anyone who challenged his winner status, painting them as losers in the public eye.

In order to understand what drives a Bullying Narcissist to assault
his victims so viciously, think back on our discussion of narcissistic
injury and how it actually makes us feel. As Dale Carnegie would
have predicted, Natalie from the last chapter experienced even well-
justified criticism as *a personal attack*; she defended herself against that
perceived attack by shifting blame, turning superior and contemptuous, or feeling indignant rage. Armstrong's behavior and public pronouncements reflect the same narcissistic strategies.

He shifts blame onto others. He hasn't done anything wrong; he's
the innocent victim of people like David Walsh, who want to destroy
his reputation.

He turns superior and contemptuous. People who question his accomplishments are envious trolls or losers, like Emma O'Reilly.

He becomes enraged when challenged. He threatens to destroy Tyler
Hamilton for testifying against him.

Though we will never get close enough to see what lies behind
them, these reactions point toward the type of core shame at the heart
of Extreme Narcissism. Armstrong's behavior suggests that whenever
his winner self-image is threatened, he feels it as a profound narcissistic injury, experienced as an attack, requiring immediate and powerful countermeasures to destroy the enemy who launched it. The
deeper a person's shame, the more likely he is to feel attacked whenever shame threatens to emerge. And the more heavily defended he is
in psychological terms, the more vicious will be his response.

"I'm a Winner and You're a Loser": The Bullying Narcissist

Through his very character, the Bullying Narcissist (like all Extreme Narcissists) devotes a huge part of his psychic energies to maintaining a *relentless narcissistic defense*, as I call it. I find the T-1000 cyborg assassin from *Terminator 2* to be a useful metaphor. If you've seen the movie, you might recall that the T-1000 is made entirely of "mimetic poly-alloy," a liquid metal that allows it to take the shape of any object it touches. Mimetic poly-alloy also means this Terminator will immediately resume its original form when "wounded" or damaged. In one famous scene, rifle shots rip huge blast holes in the T-1000's body as it runs; seconds later, the holes fill in and the fabric of its clothing appears untouched.

Like the T-1000, a person who relies on the relentless narcissistic defense is bulletproof. Criticism or defeat may briefly wound him, but he almost instantly recovers and goes on the attack. In pursuit of his winner self-image, he stands forever on guard against narcissistic injury, ready in advance to ward off criticism or other blows to his self-esteem. Like the T-1000, an Extreme Narcissist will absorb huge insults to his sense of self, instantly reconstituting the defensive character structure that protects him from shame.

It's important to bear in mind that the Bullying Narcissist consciously experiences himself to be identical with the protective shell-like character he presents to the world. It's who he is. He has no awareness that anything lies behind the relentless narcissistic defense, or that he's on the run from core shame. For this reason, the Bullying Narcissist, like other Extreme Narcissists, almost never reforms. In order to change his ways, he'd have to become a person entirely different from the one he has always felt himself to be.

YOU'RE NOT ON MY TEAM

The fact that schoolyard bullies are able to enlist other children in their campaigns at first comes as something of a surprise. Why are so many kids willing to inflict pain on one of their peers? They probably aren't all Bullying Narcissists. Some of them no doubt follow orders for fear they themselves might become targets. Others want to affiliate with a popular and socially powerful peer, thereby boosting their own status. Given that virtually everyone in middle school struggles with social anxiety to some degree, it seems likely that taking part in a bullying campaign, even if you're not the ringleader, gives you some place to locate your insecurities by identifying somebody else, not you, as the loser.

In the form of hazing rituals, bullying often occurs as a rite of passage. Fraternity and sorority pledges, rookies in the armed services, and new recruits in professional sports must often undergo experiences that shame and humiliate them, though surviving these rituals grants admission to an elite world of "winners." Particularly in sports and during wartime, victory marks the opponent as loser, thereby boosting the winning side's self-image. None of this is pathological per se, though we can see the dynamics of narcissism at work. One team builds self-esteem at the expense of the other; going down to defeat is often experienced as humiliation.

In middle school and later as an adult, the Bullying Narcissist often creates his very own "team"—at the workplace, within his family or social set—enlisting others in a joint effort to defeat and humiliate his target. While the typical middle school victim is usually a loner or marked by unfavorable difference, someone already lacking in social capital, adult targets are often highly successful. According to a study conducted by the Workplace Bullying Institute, "targets appear to be the veteran and most skilled person in the workgroup."[8]

They also tend to have better social skills and be better liked, valued for their warmth and better able to empathize. For reasons that may not be obvious, the target poses a psychological threat to the Bullying Narcissist, often because she envies that person for being admired and valued. Because she views the world through a competitive lens, the successful, highly regarded target threatens to make her feel like a comparative loser.

Experiencing the target as a threat, Bullying Narcissists will then proceed to persecute him, attempting to destroy both his reputation and his career. Like Denise in the last chapter, they may spread vicious rumors about the target. They will attempt to isolate or exclude that person from social gatherings. With a variety of techniques, they will set the target up for failure:

- Undermining or deliberately interfering with his work
- Withholding necessary information
- Persistently criticizing his work product
- Belittling his opinions
- Publicly ridiculing him

If the Bullying Narcissist is in a supervisory position, he has even greater power to sabotage his target—by establishing impossible deadlines, continually changing work guidelines for no reason, removing areas of responsibility without an explanation, et cetera.

Marie, a visitor to my website, gave me a lengthy account of being "mobbed" at the workplace. As a nursing assistant at a residential facility for disabled adults, she was at first regarded as the "star" of her unit, valued for her empathic connection with residents and praised by management for her work ethic. But when one resident asked for and received permission to transfer to Marie's unit, the nurse in charge of the unit he left behind felt slighted. Her name was Lorraine, and she began to disparage Marie to their colleagues, calling her "stuck-up." She suggested that Marie's popularity among the residents was due to seductive, unprofessional behavior.

Over time, Lorraine enlisted other employees in her vendetta. They ridiculed Marie in her presence, refused to offer support when she needed it, and forced her to assume more than her share of the workload. They lied about her to management, calling her "lazy" and accusing her of stealing food and supplies from the facility. Lorraine persecuted anyone who befriended Marie. The bullying campaign went on for months. Like many victims of workplace bullying, Marie eventually became so traumatized by the experience that she quit her job.

The emotional consequences to the workplace target closely resemble those experienced by the victim in middle school. She may come to feel helpless, vulnerable, and isolated. She may lose her self-confidence. As a result of low morale, she may be unable to concentrate, and her work product suffers. Over time, she may eventually succumb to depression, losing interest in activities she once found enjoyable. Compounding her distress may be feelings of shame about her reactions, as if she's a loser, too weak to stand up for herself. Victims of workplace bullying often blame themselves for what has occurred.

How to Cope with the Bullying Narcissist

In constant flight from loser status, engaged in a relentless narcissistic defense against feelings of core shame, Bullying Narcissists are not only dangerous but largely immune to reason or pleas for sympathy. In order to empathize with the suffering they cause their victims, they would have to "own" the shame they have projected, something they almost never do. In many cases, the best response to their behavior is to get as far away as possible. As one site visitor reported, she told her psychologist about the bullying she experienced at the hands of her boss and received the following advice: "Polish your résumé."

In middle school, escape is usually impossible unless the parents can transfer their child to another school. Day after day, the child must confront the Bullying Narcissist and her collaborators in the classroom, on the playground, in the cafeteria, or on the school bus. The inability to escape from persecution makes middle school bullying especially toxic and helps to explain the alarming number of suicides committed each year by victims of bullying.[9] Intervention by concerned parents often makes matters worse. Teachers and administrators have traditionally tried to avoid confronting the problem, although, due to persistent efforts to raise awareness, an increasing number of schools have instituted a zero tolerance policy when it comes to bullying. By and large, coping with the Bullying Narcissist in middle and high school depends upon a change in social perspective within the environment at large.

Bullying Narcissists sometimes show up in your family, too, causing feuds and building alliances against you. In those cases, "transferring" to another family obviously isn't an option. As always when dealing with an Extreme Narcissist, you need to bear in mind that shame and humiliation are the issue, even if you can't see them. Innocent remarks may be felt as grave insults. When envy comes into play, you often can't help but cause offense if you're successful, more fortunate, better looking, et cetera. You may be experienced as superior and arrogant, regardless of what you do. To reiterate, appeals to reason have little effect. The words "I didn't mean it that way" or "I do *not* think I'm better than you!" mean little to a Bullying Narcissist.

Although it may seem like "cowardly" advice, the best way of coping with the narcissist you know is often to mollify and make him feel safe, to avoid saying anything or acting in ways that may stir up shame, regardless of your intent. Bear in mind that the Bullying Narcissist is dangerous, capable of inflicting serious harm, and for this reason he or she needs to be treated with great care. You also need to remember that the Bullying Narcissist, like all Extreme Narcissists, almost never enters psychotherapy and rarely changes. Don't deceive yourself that you can persuade him or her to change.

We'll discuss much more about all these issues in Chapter Eleven.

4

"YOU'RE EVERYTHING I ALWAYS/NEVER WANTED TO BE"

The Narcissistic Parent

We've all met them before—the proud parents who brag so regularly about a son or daughter that they become overbearing. They idealize their children and seem to believe they can do no wrong, which of course means that they, the parents, must be doing a superlative job in rearing them. They often live vicariously through their children, too, basking in the reflected glow of straight-A report cards, victory in athletic or musical competitions, near-perfect SAT scores. Their boasting can sometimes make us doubt ourselves, as if we must be comparatively inferior parents.

To take pride in a son or daughter is one thing, to seek vicarious fulfillment of one's own grandiose self-image through them quite another. Idealizing children also does them a great disservice. They may never develop a realistic sense of self with a respect for their own limits or a proper regard for the feelings of others. Throughout their lives, they may also feel compelled to go on proving that they are winners. When we see mothers and fathers idealizing their children, failing to set appropriate limits or correct their bad behavior, we usually feel that those parents aren't "doing their job."

Mothers and fathers who idealize their children, exploiting them for narcissistic gain, are the subject of this chapter. To understand such parental narcissism and why it is so harmful, both to their children and sometimes to the other parents with whom they compete, we first need to be clear on what parents *ought* to provide, at different stages of life, if their children are to grow and thrive as individuals.

There's a time in a child's life when it seems entirely appropriate to be idealized. Consider the ecstatic way that new parents react when their babies reach developmental milestones, such as rolling over, learning to crawl, the first word baby speaks or the first step she takes. Parents greet each one with joyful amazement, as if it were an event of earth-shattering importance rather than maturation in the due course of things. Think about infatuated mothers cooing and smiling at their babies. Or how adults who once made intelligent conversation on topics of general interest can now talk of nothing but their child. They take immense pleasure in sharing the latest photos and obviously feel (whatever they may consciously know) that theirs is the most beautiful baby ever to be born.

During the earliest months of life, a baby occupies the adored center of her universe, exerting a profound gravitational pull upon parents in orbit around her. Not every baby is fortunate enough to have this experience, but it seems right and appropriate that she should, as if love-struck parents somehow conform to Winnicott's built-in blueprint for normality. If they are to thrive, human infants *need* to feel that they are beautiful and important during their early development;

the joyful adoration parents express would seem to provide a kind of emotional sustenance necessary for optimal growth.

Recent advances in developmental neuroscience bear this out. Most of us tend to assume that the infant's brain is fully formed upon birth, but, in fact, it continues to develop and grow throughout the first year of life. According to the psychiatrist and neurobiologist Allan Schore, neurotransmitters released during joyful interaction between mother and child promote interconnections between nerves that are necessary for the brain to develop as nature intended.[1] We might say that human babies are genetically programmed to *expect* a joyful relationship with their caretakers. Their brains depend upon it to grow, just as their bodies need key nutrients in order to thrive on a purely physiological level.

As we saw in the last chapter, infantile experience that conforms more or less to this expectation promotes a healthy sense of self and self-worth; but if it falls far short of what is needed, it leaves behind a sense of internal defect or ugliness, what I have referred to as core shame. Brain scans of children brought up in highly dysfunctional families show stunted growth and fewer neural interconnections compared to children reared in healthier environments—the anatomical expression of core shame. Extreme Narcissism, as I have said, is a defensive response to this excruciatingly painful awareness of internal defect. Without the kind of joyful relationships babies need to thrive, they may develop a defensive identity meant to disguise (from themselves and others) the profound shame they feel at their core.

At some point in their child's development, besotted parents need to temper their uncritical admiration and begin to take a more realistic view. As he learns to crawl and then walk, exploring an ever larger space, the child needs to understand that not everything he does is a cause for joy. Because the world is a hazardous place, it is crucial that he recognize his own vulnerability and limitations. Though he may heedlessly chase that ball into the street, parents must help him understand the danger posed by passing cars. He may feel omnipotent, living at the center of his parents' emotional universe, but in fact he's a small and relatively helpless human being.

The growing child must also adapt to the demands of external reality. Praise is no longer given as a matter of course, no matter what he does, as if he were perfect; now he has to earn it by living up to expectations. *Good! You used your words this time instead of hitting.* While the foundations of self-esteem are laid within the context of a loving, joyful, and largely uncritical relationship during the earliest months of life, as time goes on, earning praise from his parents for *meeting their expectations* becomes increasingly important for a child's sense of self-worth.

Parents must teach their children the rules and standards for acceptable behavior within the larger social context, and often this means frustrating them. *No, it's Ashton's turn—you have to wait. No, you can't take away Nikki's Legos just because you want them.* Babies may need to feel that their emotional experience is of paramount importance, but at some point they must learn that other people have feelings, too. In order to survive as a member of society, they *need* to learn it. Under the less-adoring, more realistic guidance of their parents, children become less egocentric and develop the ability to empathize with other people.

When it comes to building self-esteem in a child, parents thus face two more or less sequential challenges: first, to *encourage* a kind of grandiosity—making that child feel as if she is the most important person in the world—and then to *discourage* it, teaching her that she is one of many, subject to the same demands and restrictions as every-one else. Of course it's important that parents continue to make their child feel she is loved unconditionally for *who she is*, but that doesn't mean uncritical acceptance of *everything she does*.

As they grow older, children need their parents to establish clear limits, standards, and expectations for their behavior. Just as joyful admiration helped them to thrive as infants, in later years parental approval and disapproval—lovingly but firmly expressed—enable them to mature and feel good about themselves. According to the blueprint for normality, they both need and expect to have parents who exercise such benign authority at this later stage. Perhaps we might say that healthy self-esteem depends upon receiving uncondi-tional *love* and conditional *approval*, based upon a clear set of values.

Contrary to what the self-esteem movement has taught over the last thirty-odd years, children whose parents don't establish objective standards for performance and who praise everything they do will *not* develop authentic feelings of self-worth. This is especially true for children whose parents fulfill their own grandiose self-image through their "perfect" offspring. These children may grow up with an inflated sense of self-importance, entitled to have what they want and appar-ently indifferent to the consequences of their behavior, but at base, they don't actually feel good about themselves.

Like children whose earliest experience involved emotional trauma, children whose parents continue to idealize, spoil, and over-protect them are also plagued by unconscious shame: Because they receive love and admiration for living up to their parents' ideal-ized expectations, they come to feel that their true, imperfect, and "merely" human self is unacceptable—that is, shameful—and must therefore be kept hidden from view. Whatever their conscious experience, they understand that the inflated self-image they must sustain is *false*, and for this reason, they fear exposure.

Hans Christian Andersen's tale of the emperor's new clothes captures this psychological dynamic. Two swindlers come to court and persuade the vain king to let them make him a suit of clothes that will be invisible to people unfit for their positions or who are "hopelessly stupid." Made from the finest, rarest fabric, the new king's suit will be superior to all others, they tell him. Spectators are then faced with a choice: either pretend they can see the suit, or admit that they don't, thereby acknowledging their own stupidity or incompetence. You know how the story ends. The illusory suit, so elegant and superior, turns out to be an elaborate hoax. When the king is exposed as a pretentious fool, he is flooded with shame.

Parents who idealize their children don't necessarily come from families where they themselves were spoiled or idealized. Many people from highly dysfunctional or traumatic backgrounds, afflicted with core shame on an unconscious level, make use of their children to feel better about themselves. In her classic book on the subject, *The Drama of the Gifted Child*, Alice Miller first drew attention to the plight of children raised by such "insecure" mothers.

Miller describes women who relied upon their children to maintain what she refers to as their *narcissistic equilibrium*: "Quite often I have been faced with patients who have been praised and admired for their talents and their achievements. . . . In my work with [these people], I found that every one of them has a childhood history that seems significant to me: There was a mother who at the core was emotionally insecure, and who depended for her narcissistic equilibrium on the child behaving, or acting, in a particular way."[2]

Take Celine, for example, who grew up with such a narcissistic mother. For as long as she could remember, she'd been struggling to meet her mother's expectations for the person she ought to be. Only when her mother finally died did she feel truly free to be herself.

"YOU'RE THE ONE WITH ALL THE TALENT"

To this day, Celine dislikes the taste of sweets because they remind her of the "pageant crack" her mother forced her to down—Pixy Stix and sweetened energy drinks to keep her alert during competition. Mom began entering Celine in child beauty pageants not long after she turned four; most of Celine's earliest childhood memories involve grueling rehearsals under Mom's exacting gaze, long drives and cheap motels at the pageant locations, stressed-out exchanges backstage with Mom demanding she go through her routine one more time.

At age seven, when Celine began to exhibit signs of depression and an eating disorder, the doctors strongly advised Mom to pull her from the pageant circuit, and Dad finally put his foot down. A self-absorbed man who worked long hours, he normally let Mom have her way when it came to parenting decisions, but now medical authority gave him some support. He'd always objected to the expense of these pageants, and how much time he had to spend alone at home on weekends when Mom and Celine traveled. Her parents loudly feuded about whether Celine should continue competing, but Dad refused to keep paying for all the lessons, costumes, and hefty entrance fees.

Mom made no secret of her unhappiness about this decision, and Celine felt as if it were somehow her own fault. Though she gladly would have thrown out her trophies and burned the scrapbooks, Mom regularly pored over those old photos, sighing with a sense of injustice, as if life had cheated her. When Mom was a teenager, she had also competed in beauty pageants but never advanced farther than the semifinals at the county level. Grandma finally told her she obviously wasn't pretty or talented enough to win; she forced her to stop competing. Although it made no sense, Celine felt as if she were somehow to blame for Mom's personal disappointment and was therefore responsible for making it up to her.

Celine always brought home straight-A report cards, aware without being told that this was expected of her. She left the room whenever she heard Mom bragging to friends about those grades, or if she told stories about the old pageant days for the umpteenth time. Unlike Mom, who craved the spotlight, dominating conversations and freely voicing her opinions, as Celine grew older she came to feel deeply uncomfortable whenever she became the focus of attention. At school, she never raised her hand and felt the hot sting of embarrassment if a teacher called upon her.

Once the pageants came to an end, Mom enrolled her in piano lessons and soon had her playing for family and friends. Celine complained to her mother only once, explaining that she didn't play very well and that other people didn't really want to listen. "You play beautifully!" Mom insisted. "And I say that not just because I'm your mother. Only the other day, Sheila Wallace—you know, Jenny's mother—told me she thought you had it in you to be a concert pianist." Mom had probably said it herself and then Mrs. Wallace politely agreed.

Over the years, Mom herself took up and discarded a long string of hobbies, from landscape painting to pot throwing, but she never persisted at any one of them long enough to acquire any skill. "I'm no good," she'd tell Celine. "You're the one with all the talent." In between her enthusiasms, Mom often fell into one of her "blue funks," as she called them. Coming home from school, Celine could gauge her mother's mood from the particular silence in the house. A certain heaviness in the air, an atmosphere of gloom and neglect told Celine that her mother was upstairs in bed. She'd then carry up a tray with tea and toast, making Mom laugh with invented stories about events that day at school.

"That's my sweet girl," Mom would say with a happy sigh. "You know what's best for your poor old mother."

Mom suffered from a long string of ambiguous ailments, and after Celine's father died when she was a teenager, the job of tending to Mom fell on her shoulders—telephoning the doctors, driving her to appointments, searching for clues in their well-worn copy of the *Physicians' Desk Reference*. She lived at home during college, of course. Without quite choosing it, Celine wound up with a premed major and went on to medical school. She'd never had any clear idea about what to do with her life, and Mom seemed to want a doctor in the family.

Though adored by her patients and respected by her colleagues, Celine never enjoyed the practice of medicine. She felt exhausted by the seemingly endless stream of sick people in need of help, though deeply attuned to their suffering and compelled to offer them relief. At night, she went home feeling hollowed out, vaguely desperate. She lived alone and visited her mother several times each week. Every time Mom heard the front door closing as Celine let herself in, she'd call out, "Is that my daughter, the doctor?"

Celine grew up within the shadow of her mother's unhappiness, a tool in Mom's search for meaning and personal significance. From time to time, Celine tried to speak up for herself, but for the most part, she adapted to her mother's needs. In describing other boys and girls like Celine, Alice Miller puts it this way: The "child had an amazing ability to perceive and respond intuitively, that is, unconsciously, to this need of the mother, or of both parents, for him to take on the role that had unconsciously been assigned to him. This role secured 'love' for the child—that is, his parents' exploitation. He could sense that he was needed, and this need guaranteed him a measure of existential security."[3]

When Miller's book first appeared, it was released under the haunting title *Prisoners of Childhood*. Children who grow up with narcissistic parents often remain trapped in the relationship, unable to escape the prison of expectation and therefore unable to develop an independent sense of self. Even as adults they may live in subjugation to parental need, saddled with guilt for any disappointment they may cause, forever in search of "love" by fulfilling their special gifts or talents.

Because "existential security" depends upon sensing what other people need, the children of Narcissistic Parents often grow up to be highly empathic individuals, well attuned to the wishes and wants of those around them. They make loyal friends and sympathetic listeners, with an ever-available shoulder and a willing ear. All too often, they unwittingly choose a narcissistic spouse who makes similar use of them. And like Celine, they often end up in the helping professions. My relationship with my own mother, a minor narcissist in the scheme of things, explains much about my decision to become a therapist. At an early age, I also sensed that my role in life was to redeem her unhappiness through success.

Because Narcissistic Parents exploit their children in order to fulfill their own self-image, those children can't build authentic self-esteem. Self-absorbed and insensitive to the needs of others, these parents fail in the first of their tasks (to make their offspring feel safe and loved for *who they are*) and also in their second (to bring realistic standards and expectations to bear at the appropriate stage). They often drive their children to achieve great success, through which they find relief from their own unconscious shame.

After years of being used for her mother's narcissistic gain, Celine seemed almost selfless, devoted to the care of others, but many children reared by Narcissistic Parents often grow up to be narcissists themselves, craving admiration and indifferent to the feelings of others. Narcissism begets narcissism, as we say in my profession. The offspring of Narcissistic Parents often pursue careers that place them in the public eye—as politicians, athletes, or entertainers. Both parent and child thereby find relief from unconscious shame through attention, acclaim, and often the exercise of power.

The well-publicized story of Tiger Woods and his father, Earl, illustrates this dynamic at work. No child ends up on national television at age two, putting alongside Bob Hope, without a parent behind him pushing very hard. The legacy of shame and narcissism handed down from father to son begins with Earl's childhood.

"HE WAS GOING TO CHANGE THE WORLD"

Earl Dennison Woods was born in Manhattan, Kansas, in 1932, sixth child of his father's second marriage. According to neighbors who lived on their street, Earl's mother "kind of lost her mind," and his father was abusive.[4] This father apparently had "psychological problems" of his own—abruptly standing up and cursing during church services, for example, or exploding in rage at home.[5] There was no love lost between the parents. Earl's mother didn't respect her husband and their children didn't either. As one childhood friend put it, "There were a lot of things Earl didn't want to admit about his father, I'll tell you that."[6] Earl was only eleven when his father died.

As is often the case, this saga of generational narcissism begins with shame, rooted in familial dysfunction. At an early age, Earl began to display the narcissistic character structure we've come to recognize as a defense against shame. According to biographer Tom Callahan, "He wanted to be great. He wanted to be stupendous."[7] Earl's sister Mae told Callahan that "Earl was always searching for something he could do or be that was better than anybody else. I don't know how to explain it. He was so desperate to make his mark."[8]

Throughout his life, Earl would talk about his greatness, embellishing some of his accomplishments and completely inventing others. Callahan calls him a "world class braggart," but *liar* might be more accurate.[9] He lied about how old he was when his parents died, making himself younger so that his early self-reliance would appear more remarkable. He lied about receiving a scholarship to play baseball for Kansas State. Throughout his life, "he referred to himself alternately as 'the first black athlete in the entire conference' or 'the first black baseball player at Kansas State,' neither of which was true."[10]

When Barbara Ann Hart began dating Earl, her grandmother met him and warned her off. He's "awfully full of himself, wouldn't you say? We know he loves himself. But is there room in there for him to love you, too?"[11] The answer would appear to have been a resounding *no*: After Ann spent many years as a supportive army wife and gave Earl what he later referred to as his three "practice children," he returned from a tour in Thailand and began gaslighting her.

In the lead-up to their divorce, he waged "psychological warfare," constantly reminding Ann of her defects and shortcomings until he finally destroyed her self-confidence. Without discussing it with her in advance, he then had a lawyer friend come over and persuaded her to sign the divorce papers.

Earl had previously met a Thai woman while stationed in Bangkok and brought her back with him to America. Kultida Punsawad and Earl Woods married not long after his divorce, and on December 30, 1975, she gave birth to their only child, Eldrick Tont Woods. Almost from the time Tiger was born, Earl began grooming him for his future as a professional golfer. Earl had discovered golf late in life, not long before his twenty years of army service came to an end, but he quickly became obsessed with it. Even before Tiger could walk, Earl would strap him into a high chair in the garage so he could watch his father hit golf balls into a net.

"I never talked to Tiger like he was a kid," Earl would later say. "I never treated him as a kid."[12] Upon release from that garage high chair at ten months of age, Tiger's first act was to grab a putter and then, imitating his father's body waggle, immediately hit a ball into the net. From that point, Earl devoted himself to grooming Tiger for his future as a professional athlete. Den, the oldest child from his first marriage, put it this way: "Dad never said Tiger was the second coming of Jesus. He just said he was going to change the world."[13] Earl would later tell *Sports Illustrated* that "Tiger will do more than any other man in history to change the course of humanity."[14]

It was clear to Earl's older children that he had a special relationship with Tiger, acting more as his best friend than his father. Tiger remained the center of Earl's emotional universe, reared to be a fierce competitor and to pursue big dreams; he never learned humility or a regard for other people's feelings. He was a "solo flyer," as Den put it. "Tiger's whole world revolved around Tiger," and he never learned to value family.[15] As an adult, Tiger has no relationship with any of his half-siblings.

During an interview with the *San Francisco Examiner* when he was fourteen years old, Tiger told the reporter, "There's nothing in life that is more fun than beating everyone in the field." At twenty, on a United States Golf Association questionnaire that asked him to name his favorite athlete, he answered *None*. During a later interview, when asked about his impact on the sport of golf, he thought only of his victories and didn't see himself as a role model. "I've got my name on trophies fifty times here in the States. I think that's all right. That's a good impact, I think."

I'm a winner!

Like his father and grandfather, Tiger Woods has a bad temper and is famous for scowling, cursing, and throwing clubs on camera when his shots go awry. "In his time, he'd been known to shout, 'Tiger, you're the worst fucking golfer who ever lived!' before turning to Steve Williams to add, 'and you're the worst fucking caddie!'"[16] Considered by many to be both a "poor sport and a sore loser," he seems to experience losing as a personal insult, as if he feels entitled to win.[17] During the press conference he gave following the sex scandal that garnered international press, Woods gave the obligatory mea culpa, blaming his behavior on this sense of entitlement:

> I stopped living by the core values that I was taught to believe in. I knew my actions were wrong, but I convinced myself that normal rules didn't apply. I never thought about who I was hurting. Instead, I thought only about myself. I ran straight through the

boundaries that a married couple should live by. I thought I could get away with whatever I wanted to. I felt that I had worked hard my entire life and deserved to enjoy all the temptations around me. I felt I was entitled.[18]

From the beginning of their marriage, Tiger also showed a complete disregard for the feelings of his wife, Elin. *I never thought about who I was hurting. Instead, I thought only about myself.* He apparently didn't treat his many mistresses any better, making use of them to act out sexual fantasies that usually involved pain and degradation. Most of these women described him as remarkably cheap, too. After "dating" him for eighteen months, Jamie Jungers finally asked him for financial aid so she could move out of her apartment. "I can't," the billionaire told her, and he soon stopped calling.

Like his father, Tiger Woods also has a problematic relationship with the truth. In addition to the repeated lies he told his wife to cover his many affairs, he has also been known to embellish or completely invent stories to polish his heroic up-from-racial-discrimination image. In 1997, during an interview with Barbara Walters, he spoke of having been tied to a tree by sixth-graders and spray-painted with the word "nigger" on his first day in kindergarten. Years later when the sex scandal broke, his kindergarten teacher came forward and called Woods a liar, saying the incident had never happened.[19] He also lied to cover his tracks on the PGA circuit. At a May 2013 tournament, a Players Championship marshal accused Woods of lacking "character" after he intentionally distracted his main competitor before a key shot and then lied about it.

Although Woods said in his post-scandal press conference that he had "stopped living by the core values that [he] was taught to believe in," he had actually absorbed a very different set of values from his father's example of lying, bragging, and cheating. After abandoning his first wife, Earl repeatedly betrayed his second. Accompanying his son on the PGA Tour, he was infamous for the parade of women coming and going from his hotel room. Earl's own sister Mae once said that if he had been her husband, she would have shot him—and this from a woman who loved her brother deeply.[20]

Given Earl's view of his son as one of the most important figures in human history, and in light of the example he set for him, is it any wonder that Tiger Woods grew up feeling that the usual rules didn't apply?

Tiger Woods displays the two defining features of Extreme Narcissism—an inflated sense of self-importance and an indifference to the feelings of others—as well as most of the secondary features that flow from them: arrogance, a sense of entitlement, an exploitative attitude toward other people, et cetera. Tiger's hypercompetitive father lived out his winner self-image through his son, producing a world-class narcissist in his own image. Narcissism begets narcissism.

If you have sons or daughters who play team sports, you might have met parents like Earl in the bleachers. While deeply involved and devoted to their children, they may be overly invested in the outcome of a match. They often identify with their children as competitors, and some of them turn ugly when they find themselves on the losing side. The angry father who loudly abuses (bullies) the ref for unfavorable calls might be familiar to you. For such parents, more is on the line than mere victory in sports. On an unconscious level, going down to defeat makes one an all-around loser.

"You're Everything I Always/Never Wanted to Be": The Narcissistic Parent

Less blatant are the Narcissistic Parents who vicariously compete through their child's academic or artistic success. They shore up their own winner identity via children who are "better" than yours, though the comparison may never actually be stated. Narcissistic Parents with sufficient drive can scale great heights through their children, though you have to wonder at what emotional cost. For those children, an internalized perfectionistic parent, contemptuous of the "ordinary," would seem to be the primary psychological legacy. When parents scorn anything less than the highest levels of performance, their children will most likely grow up hating themselves for being "merely" human, contemptuous of their own limitations, and riddled with unconscious shame.

Tiger Woods's famous tendency to abuse himself for bad shots offers an example. The professional athlete needs a highly competitive spirit to succeed, of course, but if Extreme Narcissism comes into play, he will need ongoing victories to prove that he's a shame-free winner rather than a contemptible loser. When he's on top of the world and things are going his way, Tiger comes across as cocky and self-assured, fulfilling his destiny as the greatest golfer of all time. When he does badly, he becomes "the worst fucking golfer who ever lived." Like the Bullying Narcissist, at those times he also inflicts his shame or sense of defect upon others around him: Longtime loyal caddy Steve Williams becomes "the worst fucking caddie" ever.

Best or worst, winner or loser—there are only two possibilities for the Extreme Narcissist.

The Narcissistic Parent whose child provides vicarious fulfillment will often worship that child in the manner of Earl Woods. But if that child disappoints, or attempts to establish an independent identity, the Narcissistic Parent may instead turn on that child, often quite viciously. Rather than living vicariously through the child as an idealized winner, the parent may instead cast him or her into the role of contemptible loser, forcing that child to carry the burden of unconscious shame. Like the Bullying Narcissist, this type of parent boosts his or her self-esteem at the expense of the child, with devastating effects. Such children may be emotionally crippled for life, burdened with toxic levels of shame and self-loathing.

Several years ago, I wrote a post on my website titled "The Narcissistic Mother" and have since received hundreds of comments from men and women who recognized their own experience in my description. These site visitors tell harrowing stories of mothers who verbally and sometimes physically abused them, who throughout childhood told their children that they were stupid, worthless, or crazy. These mothers forced their sons and daughters to carry the burden of unconscious shame, casting their children into the role of losers within their narcissistic worldview.[21]

Narcissistic Parents often enlist other family members on their side, causing rifts and building alliances against a "bad" child. In other words, they may bully their own children. The victims of such behavior often describe themselves as a "scapegoat," held accountable for all the family troubles. Their mothers often compare them unfavorably to a sibling viewed as "golden," one child a loser and the other a winner. Narcissistic Parents tell blatant lies, too, painting themselves as victims and their children as heartless ingrates.

Celine coped with one type of Narcissistic Parent by meeting her mother's expectations; while unfulfilled and mostly unhappy as an adult, she achieved some level of success, earning affection and respect within her community though she often felt empty and isolated. With a toxic, abusive mother who cast her in the role of family scapegoat, Mora suffered more deeply and was afflicted for life with profound self-loathing. If Mora ever tried to talk to other people about the abuse, nobody would believe that a mother could behave in such ways.

"She may not express it very well," people would tell her, "but you have to know your mother loves you at heart."

DESPERATELY SEEKING APPROVAL

Mora cannot remember a time when she didn't feel as if she were a blight upon her mother's existence. Her older brother, Shane, was Mom's pride and joy, the one who could do no wrong, while Mora felt like a burden. Throughout childhood, she often heard how Dad had never wanted to have a second child and left the family not long after Mora was born. Her mother didn't actually come out and say so, but Mora felt as if her birth were the cause of her parents' divorce. Perhaps they'd still be married now if Shane had remained an only child.

Mom always made light of Shane's misbehavior. "Boys will be boys," she often said, even when she caught him stealing from the money jar in the kitchen. By contrast, she punished Mora for the smallest of infractions, or for accidents such as spilling milk at the dinner table. She demanded much more help from Mora, too, expecting her to do the laundry and most of the housework.

When Dad stopped making child-support payments and disappeared, Mom went back to work as a secretary. Not a day went by without angry complaints about the injustice of life. Because Mom so obviously felt resentful about putting dinner on the table after an "exhausting" day at the office, Mora taught herself how to cook, though

Mom didn't seem to care much for her cooking. Most nights, they ate takeout or TV dinners.

Every year, her mother staged elaborate birthday parties for Shane and usually forgot Mora's birthday. If Mom remembered to buy her a present, she usually gave items of clothing that Mora would never wear, in sizes too large or styles more appropriate for a girl half her age. On her own birthday, no matter what Mora did to make it special, Mom went into full martyr mode. Since her ne'er-do-well ex-husband had walked out, she'd sacrificed her life to motherhood . . . and what did she have to show for it? No one cared about her, especially not her ungrateful children. Mom spoke in the plural but Mora knew the criticism applied only to herself and not her brother.

Mom often made sarcastic remarks about Mora's weight, but whenever Mora went on a diet, Mom usually stocked the pantry with doughnuts and cookies. Or she'd make the unusual offer of taking Mora out for ice cream. When Mora tried losing weight as a teenager, Mom accused her of wanting to attract boys and called her a slut. If any boy asked Mora out during high school, Mom told her that he only wanted sex, then she flirted with him when he came to pick Mora up. Mora began meeting her dates away from home.

The mothers of other kids often came up to Mora at school functions, complimenting her for one award or another. "Your mother is so terribly proud—you're all she talks about!" At home, Mom called her a show-off and warned her not to get too big for her britches. If Mora told her about some special achievement, Mom usually replied, "Pride goeth before a fall." During her junior year, Mom mocked her for applying to college and said she'd never get in. Mora was accepted on scholarship to her first choice.

Shane had already moved out by that point and more or less disappeared from their lives. Now and then, he'd call in extremis and Mom would wire him the money he needed. Mom grudgingly bought Mora a few textbooks for her college courses and told all her friends she was putting her daughter through school. Mom also enrolled in community college herself and began working toward an associate's degree. At the end of each semester, she'd call Mora to compare grades. Mora finally learned she had to lie about the good marks she was earning if she didn't want Mom to attack her.

When Mora became engaged to marry Jeff, a boy she'd met as a senior in college, Mom offered no congratulations and told Mora not to expect any help with wedding expenses. She then tried to control every aspect of the reception and threw temper tantrums when she didn't get her way. She came late to the ceremony, making an attention-grabbing entrance just as the wedding march began to play.

In the early days of dating and throughout their engagement, Jeff had seemed an attentive and appreciative lover, treating her as an equal partner. As a husband, he held more archaic views. He believed that a wife owed obedience to her husband. He viewed cooking and cleaning as "woman's work," though he also expected Mora to hold down a job and pay her half of the household expenses. He insisted she have sex whether or not she felt like it—as part of her spousal duties. When Mora gave birth to a daughter, Jeff regarded diaper-changing, bathing, feeding, et cetera, as "a mother's domain."

Once, and only once, Mora complained to her mother, foolishly expecting sympathy. "Just be grateful he's still around," Mom told her. "You have no idea what a burden it is to bring up kids all alone. Don't make waves—that's my advice."

*   *   *

When people from more or less normal family backgrounds hear such accounts, they usually greet them with polite skepticism. Belief in the sanctity of a mother's love is nearly universal. As a psychotherapist, I know better. The Narcissistic Parent is incapable of empathy and unable to love. Like Earl Woods, some of these parents view their children as extensions of themselves, reflections of their own grandiosity; others resemble Mora's mother and exploit their offspring as containers for the shameful sense of defect they don't want to feel. They make themselves winners by turning their own children into losers, or they feel envious when their child succeeds.

Like many children of Narcissistic Parents, Mora loved her mother and tried desperately to win her approval. Despite all the evidence, she continued to hope that it might be possible to earn her love. She mostly blamed herself for her mother's lack of maternal feelings. Only a child so ugly and defective could account for the absence of love. Like other such unfortunate children, she also found a narcissistic partner to marry when she grew up, a man not so psychologically different from her mother. Attuned to the needs of others, deforming themselves in order to win acceptance, the children of Narcissistic Parents make natural prey for self-absorbed, exploitative narcissists like Jeff.

This account of Mora's relationship with her mother may strike some people as implausible or exaggerated, but I've heard much worse from clients and site visitors. The mother of one of my clients knowingly looked the other way while her five-year-old daughter was sexually molested by a family friend. This mother needed the man's help and she sacrificed her daughter in order to get it. Multiple visitors to my website have told of parents (usually mothers) who launched all-out vendettas against them for daring to strike out on their own.

These parents told plausible-sounding lies to family members or friends and often succeeded in alienating those people from the offending child. Many Extreme Narcissists have learned how to *appear* normal and loving to others, disguising their vicious intentions by coming across as victims of mistreatment.

How to Cope with the Narcissistic Parent

People who grew up and continue under the tyranny of a Narcissistic Parent often ask me for advice on how to cope. In the most egregious cases, I suggest severing ties or, at the very least, placing powerful limits on the relationship. The Extreme Narcissist of every stripe almost never seeks psychological treatment and rarely changes. Protecting oneself by staying as far away from them as possible often makes the most sense.

Sadly, the children of Narcissistic Parents, forever in search of parental love and blaming themselves for its absence, find this an extremely difficult thing to do. Despite what they may know, the guilt they feel for "abandoning" their parents makes them feel even more unworthy. My client whose mother traded her to a child molester still feels guilty about the infrequency of their contact, as if this makes her an "undutiful" daughter. From time to time, she can't stop herself from telephoning out of concern, only to hear herself attacked for a long list of grievances. This client's daughter finds her grandmother so emotionally repellent that she refuses to see her.

"Stop hoping she'll become the mother you always wanted," I often tell my clients. "She's incapable of loving and will never change."

Setting limits on contact is another option. One site visitor exchanges birthday cards and short visits on holidays but otherwise avoids her parents. Others establish rules for acceptable behavior and cut short their interactions if a Narcissistic Parent becomes abusive. Unfortunately, the Extreme Narcissist doesn't take well to having limits set for him and may experience the frustration of his wishes as an attack, turning vicious in response. It always saddens me that I have so little useful advice to offer in those cases. Surviving the relationship with Narcissistic Parents means protecting yourself from continuing injury by people who have no regard for you or anyone else and who disdain the conventions of ordinary civilized behavior. In my experience, that usually means severing relations.

In the context of psychotherapy, it may take years for a client to build the self-esteem and emotional strength necessary to break free. This process usually involves profound grief, as she comes to mourn the loving parent she never had.

Encounters with Narcissistic Parents who compete via their sons and daughters should be a familiar experience for readers with children of their own. These experiences are irksome more than anything else, though sometimes, if our children happen to be struggling or if we have some doubts about our own parenting skills, the gloating, triumphant parent can make us feel even worse. In these cases, it's important to recall that the Extreme Narcissist makes himself a winner at your expense, by off-loading feelings of shame and unworthiness and forcing you to carry them. As a result, without quite realizing it, you may become defensive and "fight back," engaging in a contest to prove that you are *not* the loser.

As we'll discuss in greater detail in Chapter Eleven, such a contest is fruitless. In dealing with the competitive, Narcissistic Parent, as with most Extreme Narcissists, the best course of action is to disengage.

5

"I WANT YOU TO WANT ME"
The Seductive Narcissist

Harlan was referred to me by his wife's therapist, a colleague within my professional community. Not long before he contacted me, Harlan's wife, Emily, had discovered that he was having an affair with someone they both knew well. The other woman and her husband actually lived next door to Harlan and Emily; the two couples often socialized together. They belonged to the same set, a group of young married couples, all professionals with families in a closely knit community. Harlan and Emily's marriage as well as their social life were now at risk of unraveling.

During our initial phone contact, I sensed that Harlan had no real interest in psychotherapy and was coming only because his wife had begged him to call me. "She wants me to talk about why I cheated on her," he told me over the phone. Right on time for the scheduled appointment, he showed up in my waiting room—an attractive, well-dressed man with an engaging smile. I invited him into my office.

Harlan draped his expensive-looking overcoat across the end of my couch with a gesture that seemed both self-assured and self-aware, as if he were conscious of the impression he was making. As he settled into the chair opposite my own, crossing one leg over the other, he didn't appear the least bit uncomfortable or anxious, the way most new clients do during an initial consultation. He brushed a stray thread from his pants leg.

"So, what would you like to know?" he said with a faint grin.

The first few minutes confirmed my initial impression: that Harlan didn't want psychotherapy. He was here at his wife's behest and intended to cooperate, but he had no real interest in exploring the reasons for the affair. I suspected that we would meet for a few sessions at most. I spent most of that hour asking Harlan questions; he willingly answered them all and spoke with surprising candor. He maintained good eye contact. He seemed to enjoy having such an interested spectator to his life and obviously aimed to please. Though he had no real interest in my professional insights, he gave me his full attention and was clearly exerting his energies to be engaging.

He was "done" with Emily—that's the way he put it. He said that he felt badly but couldn't help it. After seven years of marriage, he felt bored and stifled. His tone suggested that his feelings were completely understandable, as if I would naturally sympathize. Marilyn, the next-door neighbor, had been a distraction. In retrospect, he probably should have looked farther afield (appealing bad-boy grin), but, then, he hadn't expected the affair to be discovered. Only a spot of very bad luck had brought it to light: Marilyn's husband had unexpectedly returned home when a canceled flight led him to abort a business trip. He had caught them in the act.

When Harlan told me about the discovery, he gave me a complicit smile, as if I, too, would find it an amusing contretemps. He seemed to take special pleasure in using the phrase *in flagrante delicto*. As much as I disapproved of his behavior, I found him personally appealing—in spite of myself.

He didn't mention his children, aged two and four. When I finally asked how he thought a divorce would affect them, he shrugged. "They'll live. It happens all the time."

In answer to my next question, he told me that the affair with Marilyn hadn't been his first. On his business travels, he regularly met and bedded other women. He'd fooled around with several women at the office.

"I can seduce anyone," he told me with obvious pride, going on to explain his methods. It all boiled down to one simple rule: *Make them feel good about themselves.* Listen closely and maintain eye contact, ask a lot of questions, behave as if you're truly fascinated by what they have to say.

"Kind of like what you do," he said with a grin.

During that consultation, I felt as if he were attempting to seduce me, too—inviting me to admire his style and success with women, to *like* him in a way, though I knew he had absolutely no interest in me as a person or professional. I was his audience.

After our appointment was over, I never saw Harlan again.

"NOBODY ELSE IN THE WORLD MATTERED, AT LEAST FOR THAT MOMENT"

I can seduce anyone.

Over the years, those words have stayed with me. I've met other people who have reminded me of Harlan, men and women who possess a certain personal allure that makes them almost irresistible, at least when they're trying to win you over. No doubt you've met such people, too. They can "light up the room," as the expression goes. They're "magnetic" individuals, exerting an ineluctable pull on our interest. We often want their attention, and when we get it, we feel flattered.

Charisma.

Not everyone who possesses charisma is an Extreme Narcissist, but many charismatic individuals lack genuine empathy for other people and are driven by an inflated sense of self-importance, even though they may not necessarily come across as egotistical. On the contrary, many of them, like Harlan, have a special ability to make *other people* feel important, and they exploit their skill in the service of manipulation. By bestowing attention, the Seductive Narcissist makes his target feel so good about herself that she wants even more contact. Despite herself, she may want to *submit.*

Some memorable American politicians have possessed this same quality, and it has helped them to inspire loyalty. Franklin Delano Roosevelt and Ronald Reagan have both been described as charismatic leaders. People who have met Bill Clinton, even those predisposed to dislike him, come away from contact impressed with his personal magnetism. When asked to account for Clinton's charisma, observers often cite the fact that he "gives everyone he meets his full, undivided attention."[1] They bring up the intense eye contact, the way Clinton makes them feel that nobody else in the world matters just then. He also gives the impression that he *cares.* Through his focus and attention, he forges an empathic link with the other person, making him or her feel special, at the center of his emotional universe . . . at least for the moment.

"I Want You to Want Me": The Seductive Narcissist

I'm not equating charisma with narcissism. Many or even most charismatic politicians may actually care, but Seductive Narcissists only simulate empathy. They intuitively understand, or have learned over time, what makes other people "tick," and they use that knowledge to manipulate them. Boosting self-esteem is their particular métier. Most of us wish to feel that we're fascinating people, worthy of attention and interest. Most of us enjoy it when another person enters into our feelings and validates them. Of course we do. In granting our wish, the Seductive Narcissist invites us to join with him in a mutual admiration society. He holds us with his fascinated gaze, compelling us to return the admiration.

In other words, the Seductive Narcissist appeals to our own narcissism in order to get what he wants from us. The bargain is implicit, unspoken: *I will make you feel that you're an exceptionally fascinating person, eminently desirable, if you agree to feel the same way about me.* In contrast to the Bullying Narcissist who off-loads his shame and then strives to make you feel bad about yourself, the Seductive Narcissist wants to boost your self-esteem. He wants you to feel like a winner so that you'll see him as a winner, too. You often don't realize it until it's too late, but his interest and admiration is feigned while yours is quite genuine.

In the harrowing account of her marriage to and divorce from a Seductive Narcissist, Tina Swithin describes the intoxication of being "swept off her feet by a modern day Prince Charming."[2] Immediately after she met Seth but before they'd even gone out together, he bought her a full-day package at a local spa because she "deserved" to be pampered. He sent her flowers at work with a note that read "I hope your day is as beautiful as you are." In a phone call before their first date, he told her "that there was something fundamentally wrong with any man who would allow a woman pay for dinner."[3]

In the first of her "Red Flag Reflections" on her relationship with Seth, Tina recalls wondering at the time whether he was too good to be true. Of course he was! She and Seth had only just met, but already he claimed to know that she "deserved" pampering. He told her she was beautiful. He promised never to let her pay. All this from a complete stranger . . . and yet it was entirely seductive. Seth made Tina feel as if she were a beautiful and rare individual, deserving special treatment. He implicitly promised to take care of her. And, not surprisingly, she fell in love with him.

In many ways, romantic love is a semidelusional state of mind in which two people agree that they are the most attractive, fascinating people in the world. They become the center of one another's universe. Only during infancy, when our parents (hopefully) bestow uncritical adoration upon us, does another person view us in the same besotted way, as if we are perfect. Infatuation is a heady brew, and when two people mutually idealize one another, it can feel like bliss. A Seductive Narcissist like Seth understands and exploits the implicit bargain involved in romantic love, even if the exploitation isn't fully conscious. He worships the other in order to stimulate adoration.

It's probably too much to ask of any person embarking on romance to preserve a modest, realistic view of who one really is. It feels wonderful to hear you're so very special that you deserve to be pampered, even if you ought to know you're no more deserving than anyone else. It feels wonderful to receive flowers and be told you're beautiful, to hear that you'll be taken care of.

Tina had every reason to be suspicious, to doubt Seth's sincerity, but she wanted to believe what he told her. She wanted to see herself as the person he was describing. Seth appealed to Tina's narcissism and invited her to idealize him in return. As with many such Seductive Narcissists, Seth's admiration for Tina lasted only as long as she viewed him uncritically. Years later, when she filed for divorce, he turned vicious and tried to destroy her, displaying the characteristics of a Vindictive Narcissist—the subject of Chapter Nine.

My client Julia, another Seductive Narcissist, used similar tactics with the men she dated, though she never turned vicious. When the admiration drug began to wear off or if the man wanted too much from her, she simply dropped him.

THE HEARTBREAKER

In the beginning of our work together, it was difficult to understand exactly why Julia had come for treatment. She complained of a vague feeling of emptiness. While she could see that the people around her enjoyed many aspects of their lives, she told me that she found pleasure in almost nothing. She had never consciously felt depressed, though life often struck her as pointless. In my experience, people usually seek professional help when emotional pain has become unbearable. Julia instead seemed bored.

She was a beautiful young woman in her mid-twenties, a British national living temporarily in the United States. She usually came to her sessions directly from the law office where she worked as a front-desk receptionist—a kind of human ornament, as she described herself—so when I saw her, she was of course well dressed, her makeup perfect, every hair in place. On the rare occasions when a session took place on a day off, she looked no different. She told me that many lawyers at the firm had asked her out on dates, and I found it easy to believe. With her British accent, her beauty, and her quiet air of sophistication, she was thoroughly charming.

Julia obviously didn't earn much as a receptionist but that didn't curtail her lifestyle: She never lacked for men eager to escort her to expensive restaurants. They took her to the theater and the ballet, too, or away for spa weekends. Julia had learned that, for a certain type of man, she was the perfect companion, a woman who completed his self-image. With a beautiful, charming woman on his arm, he knew he'd appear dynamic and successful. Other men would view him as a winner. They might feel envious, too, wondering what it would be like in bed with Julia.

As far as bed was concerned, Julia made her dates feel like amazing sexual athletes. Though she admitted to me that she had never experienced orgasm except through masturbation, she told each of her men that he was the very first to bring her such pleasure. She wasn't lacking in experience, she freely admitted, but no man before him had ever managed to bring her to the point of release. In the beginning of her "relationships," Julia often came across as insatiable, though, in fact, she had little interest in sex.

In my description, Julia comes across as selfish and conniving—which of course, she was—but during her sessions, she didn't usually strike me that way. She seemed to be operating by instinct, not consciously intent on exploiting these men but compelled to do so by some inner need. She didn't plot her actions in advance or scheme to get what she wanted. She actually seemed to have no goals at all. At the most essential level, her entire personality seemed geared toward evoking desire in men. She wasn't overtly flirtatious, but when she fixed a man with her gaze and gave him her full attention, she had an innate ability to make him feel important.

Julia sometimes had a similar effect on me, too, though I understood myself and her dynamics well enough to recognize the pattern.

As our work progressed, she became increasingly vivacious and entertaining, sharing vivid accounts of her exploits. When I offered my insights, she often responded with deep appreciation, as if I were the most amazing therapist in the world! Without quite knowing that she was doing it, Julia wanted to make me feel good about myself . . . and hungry for more contact with the woman who made me feel that way. I never forgot that, at some level, she was deeply unhappy and that her seductiveness was likely a defense against some unconscious pain we hadn't yet reached.

It should come as no surprise that a man she dated would often fall in love with Julia. It seemed almost predictable that he would eventually insist upon a reassurance that they were "exclusive." Several asked her to move in and offered to support her. A couple of them even proposed marriage. At that point, when the man wanted to take possession, Julia would cut him loose. She wouldn't do it in a cruel way. Instead, she'd use the obvious excuses to break it off: *I'm too young. I'm not ready for marriage. I'm only in the States temporarily so it makes no sense to get serious.* Julia broke many a heart.

While most of the Extreme Narcissists I've described so far came from unstable, often violent backgrounds, Julia's childhood was marred by a single traumatic event. When she was only six years old, her parents had traveled abroad on a kind of second honeymoon, during which her mother was killed in an automobile collision. Although the father survived, he went into a deep mourning that lasted several years. Theirs had been a happy marriage. Julia found herself in the care of a long succession of nannies while her father disappeared into his grief. He eventually remarried when Julia was in her teens but she never took to her stepmother, usually referring to her as "that fat cow Ellen."

My work with Julia lasted less than a year. We'd made some limited progress in exploring the motives for her seductiveness when she decided to return to London. Although I suggested that she might be in flight from our deepening work, afraid to face her pain, she made some persuasive arguments about why it made pragmatic sense to go home. Her words reminded me of the reasons she gave to her suitors when she cut them loose. As we shook hands and said goodbye at the end of our final session, she expressed warm gratitude for my help and said she'd miss me. I felt sad to see our work come to an end.

It would be overly simplistic to make a cause-and-effect explanation, as if the death of her mother fully accounts for Julia's narcissistic behavior later in life. And yet, this tragic early loss must have played an important part. She learned early on that people you love can abruptly vanish; perhaps it's better not to let them matter in the first place, better not to let yourself need them. Maybe you can avoid feeling helpless and at risk by inspiring desire in *other* people. When you later abandon them, *they* will be the ones to feel hurt and helpless, not you.

The Bullying Narcissist off-loads shame and forces his victims to carry it for him, proving himself a winner by triumphing over the loser. The Seductive Narcissist projects need and desire onto other people, making herself feel powerful, almost invincible in the process. By appealing to the narcissism of her dates, making them feel like superior sexual athletes, Julia evoked intense desire. On the receiving end of their adoration, Julia confirmed her superior, invulnerable sense of self. Although she didn't use the word, I'm sure she also saw herself as a winner. When she spoke of these men, I often detected a note of contempt in the background, as if they were weak, vain, and easily manipulated—*losers*.

On an unconscious level, the Seductive Narcissist is also in flight from core shame—the sense that one's development has gone awry, leaving behind a felt conviction that there is something *wrong* inside. It is definitely *not* in the general order of things to lose your mother when you're only six and for your father to abandon you emotionally for years thereafter. I see the psychological fallout from such a traumatic loss as *shame*, but I suspect this view might at first seem puzzling.

In his essential book about shame and pride, Donald Nathanson defines shame as a kind of disappointed expectation, where a *positive affect* (say, interest or pleasure) is interrupted and cut short.[4] Nathanson writes for a largely professional audience, and his book is steeped in the sometimes arcane language of affect theory. To understand what he means by describing shame as the interruption of positive affect, consider the following passage from *Anna Karenina*.

Kitty and Vronsky are dancing together at a ball. Kitty believes herself to be in love with Vronsky and, until this moment, has thought the feeling was reciprocated: "Kitty looked into his face, which was so close to her own, and long afterwards—for several years after—that look, full of love, to which he made no response, cut her to the heart with an agony of shame." So when Kitty gazes lovingly into the face of Vronsky and he doesn't reciprocate it, the experience leaves her with a lasting sense of shame.

Since I first read this passage, I've come to think of core shame as a kind of unrequited love. Perhaps you've had the experience of loving someone, possibly even declaring your love, only to find that the other person didn't return it. Perhaps you have felt the particular humiliation of being told "I just want to be friends." Afterward, you might have wanted to keep it a secret from your friends, for fear that they'd view you with pity or, even worse, with superior amusement, glad not to be in your shoes.

To feel a joyful, loving interest in another person only to find it unreciprocated is an agonizing experience. A famous video clip commonly referred to as the "Still Face Experiment" poignantly illustrates just how distressing that experience can be. If you haven't seen it before, I urge you to view it now—it's available on YouTube. Just as Kitty's loving gaze is met by Vronsky's indifference, the baby's smiles and gestures elicit no response from its mother; the baby is clearly distraught. In the language of affect theory, when the infant's positive affect (what Nathanson refers to as *interest-excitement* or *enjoyment-joy*) is disrupted by the mother's failure to reciprocate, the result is the affect *shame-humiliation*. You might instead view the baby's experience as mere frustration, which of course it is, but bear in mind that frustration implies a disappointed expectation—as in "I'm frustrated that I can't learn this material as easily as I expected."

If we could put the baby's preverbal experience into words, we might express it this way: *Why isn't Mama returning my smile? This feels really bad. Did I do something wrong to make her stop giving me that special look of joy?* Children very often blame themselves for parental failures, as if they are unloved because they themselves have done something wrong or because they are fundamentally unlovable. All mothers naturally love their children—of course they do!—so if your own lacks maternal feeling, you must be to blame. Children often blame themselves when a parent dies, too, even though there is no rational foundation for such a belief. They may feel that their parent died because they are very bad and undeserving.

Returning to Julia, then, her mother's untimely death was the ultimate interruption of positive affect, instilling her with core shame. Julia may have felt responsible for her mother's death, too, as if such a tragic loss could only be "explained" by her own unworthiness. In order to ward off this painful (and largely unconscious) sense of defect, Julia rejected her own needy, vulnerable self and developed the sort of defensive narcissistic personality we have come to recognize. She clearly lacked empathy for any of her "victims." And while not overtly grandiose, she felt a quiet kind of superiority that entitled her to exploit them for whatever she wanted.

Tragic early loss may shed light on another celebrity often described as a narcissist. When she was only five years old, pop icon Madonna lost her own mother. Her life story since then includes the seduction of many men and women she found useful, followed by an unfeeling rejection once she had finished with them.

NARCISSIST IN A MATERIAL WORLD

After she became famous, Madonna would say, "we are all wounded in one way or another by something in our lives, and then we spend the rest of our lives reacting to it or dealing with it or trying to turn it into something else." For Madonna, the anguish of losing her mother "left me with a certain kind of loneliness and an incredible longing for something." She has also said, "If I hadn't had that emptiness, I wouldn't have been so driven. Her death had a lot to do with me saying—after I got over the heartache—I'm going to be really strong if I can't have my mother, I'm going to take care of myself."[5]

According to object relations theory, narcissistic people find the experience of need and dependency to be unbearable; as a result, they develop a set of psychological defenses that embody an extreme form of *anti*-dependency.[6] *I don't need anyone. I can take care of myself because I already have what I need.* In the passage above, Madonna seems to acknowledge that the unbearable loss of her mother fueled her ambitious drive to become famous. We can imagine how painfully helpless she felt, losing her mother at age five. Reacting against that pain, in an effort to escape from feeling small and helpless, Madonna vowed to "rule the world" instead.[7]

While object relations theory focuses on issues of need and dependency to account for narcissism, we are nonetheless in the realm of shame: Seductive Narcissists often identify their feelings of need or longing as *the source of their shame*. On an unconscious (and sometimes conscious) level, they dread the experience of emotional dependency. Rather than feeling needy or dependent, the Seductive Narcissist strives to make other people want her instead, both to rid herself of unbearable desire but also to manipulate and control them.

My client Julia exploited the men she dated for the lifestyle they afforded, far beyond her personal means. Madonna made use of people, mostly men, to further her vast ambitions. Often she became lovers with a man when their careers dovetailed and he could help her to advance. In early 1980, not long after Madonna had abandoned her ambition to become a dancer, Dan Gilroy welcomed her into his bed, his heart, and his band. From Dan, Madonna gained some basic knowledge about musical instruments and how to sing in front of an audience with musicians behind her. Then she dumped him and started her own band . . . without Dan.

"It was pretty tough being her boyfriend, to say the least," Gilroy later commented, "mostly because you knew there was no way she was going to be faithful. She always had a lot of other guys lined up, and each one had a purpose in her life. When she was done with me that time, well, she was done with me for good."[8] Mark Kamins, a later boyfriend, introduced Madonna to a young executive at Warner Bros. Records and helped her secure her first recording contract with the understanding that he would produce the album. Instead, she went with a more established producer and dumped Kamins.

Erica Bell describes Madonna's modus operandi in blunt terms. Bear in mind that this description comes from a longtime friend, not a rejected lover or an enemy. "She seduces people," Bell says. "She'll tell you what you want to hear, she flatters you, kisses your ass, makes you feel a part of her life. She's a smart girl. She knows how to get her way. . . . Then, after she has you set up the right way, she sucks it all out of you."[9] After Gilroy and Kamins, Madonna hooked up with John "Jellybean" Benitez, an influential DJ in Manhattan who put some final touches on her first album and added the song "Holiday." They became lovers. Then they became engaged.

In the middle of their engagement, Madonna began dating Steve Newman, the editor of a small but influential magazine in New York. After he featured Madonna on the cover of *Fresh 14*, they began a sexual relationship. When Newman told her that he didn't want to become romantically involved if she wasn't going to be committed to him, she gave him the reassurance he needed (though still engaged to Benitez). "Oh yeah, definitely," she told him. "I want this relationship more than anything in the world."[10] Jealous and full of rage, Benitez spent an entire evening trying to track down his fiancée and finally found her at Newman's home. He broke in and caused a violent scene.

According to Newman, Madonna and Benitez then had a vicious

argument. She was screaming at him, saying things like "If it wasn't for me, you'd be nobody today. I *made* you, Jellybean. You were just nothing until I came along and fucking transformed your life."[11] After Benitez finally left, Madonna begged Newman's forgiveness and said she loved him, and *only* him. A few months later, however, after success was finally coming her way, she informed him that the relationship was over. "You're this nobody writer making no money. Right? But I'm *Madonna*. I mean, I'm making, what? A quarter of a million a year? And next year, I'll be making ten times that much."

"Is that all it's about with you?" Newman asked. "Success and money?"

"Yeah, it is," she answered. "Now that you mention it, it is."

Madonna biographer J. Randy Taraborrelli explains that by this time, "every step of her career was a seduction—one person after another being seduced by her to do her bidding."[12] She didn't confine her seductions to members of the opposite sex. One-time manager Camille Barbone was among the first to recognize Madonna's immense talent and to predict her meteoric rise to stardom. She signed Madonna to her agency, gave her a weekly allowance, rented her an apartment, and likely fell in love with her. Madonna gave Barbone the impression that the feeling was reciprocated, though the two never had sexual relations.

"She seduced me, psychologically," Barbone says.[13] "She soaks up what she can and drains you in every way and then goes on to her next victim." Barbone believes that Madonna "wasn't intentionally malicious, but just incapable of seeing life from anyone else's point of view. She wanted what she wanted, and if you didn't give it she turned her back on you." Although Barbone still sounds bitter many years after Madonna broke their contract and dropped her, her comments shed compassionate light on the origins of the star's drive:

> It all has to do with her mother, it all goes back to her death. It has to do with Madonna feeling so beat up by what she felt when her mother died, she never wanted to connect to her emotions. So, she leaves people before they can leave her, the way her mother did. . . . Her mother, that's what it's always been about.[14]

When my client Julia was six years old, her mother died in a car accident. Madonna's mother died of breast cancer when her daughter was only five. Though the origins of narcissism can't be traced to one consistent family background, a surprising number of Extreme Narcissists have experienced some kind of early trauma or loss. As we saw in Chapter Three, Lance Armstrong's father abandoned him when he wasn't quite three years old. The parents of Steve Jobs, as we shall see in Chapter Seven, put him up for adoption as an infant and walked away—a fact that friends and biographers say explains a great deal about his narcissistic personality.

Although Madonna comes across as cold, ruthless, and manipulative in these accounts, she actually believed herself to be in love with many of the people she exploited. Unlike my client Julia, who felt largely indifferent to the men she dated, Madonna easily grew infatuated with someone new (and just as easily became disillusioned or bored). Many Seductive Narcissists fall head over heels in love with someone they perceive to be an ideal mate, a partner to complement their idealized self-image, and then fall out of love once the imperfections begin to show.

This kind of romantic love reflects little real awareness or understanding of the other person. Because they lack empathy and because they often force other people to carry unwanted shame or desire, all Extreme Narcissists find it difficult to recognize other people as separate individuals with an interior life of their own. Even when they fall in love, they experience the love object more as a reflection upon themselves than as a separate person. They tend to idealize the other, at least temporarily, and expect to be idealized in return.

You're perfect, and your love for me confirms that I'm perfect. Together, we are perfect.

In the beginning of their relationship, it's quite possible that Seth, Tina Swithin's narcissistic suitor, believed himself to be in love with her. He saw her as beautiful, deserving, and exceptional; the fact that she came to adore him in return then confirmed his own idealized self-image. The ideal doesn't really exist, of course, and reality inevitably breaks through over time. For most of us, idealized romantic love in the early stages then evolves into a more realistic kind of love based on a fuller knowledge of the other person, imperfections and all. For the Seductive Narcissist, once the flaws become apparent, love may abruptly give way to indifference, scorn, or even hatred.

Even then, the Seductive Narcissist can't see the other person in realistic terms, as a separate and unique individual. Instead of seeing her as "all good," he may come to view her as "all bad"—a shame-ridden loser—shifting her from pedestal to trash heap.

You may have friends who go from one relationship to another, falling abruptly in love with some fabulous new flame, only to become disillusioned a few weeks later. They may at first speak in glowing terms of the new lover and then later with contempt once the affair has ended. Sometimes these people go through bipolarlike phases, beginning a new romance with manic intensity and slipping into depression when it falls apart. If it's the other person who walks away, the serial romantic may then feel like a loser, and his or her depression usually has a component of core shame. The serial romantic isn't always an Extreme Narcissist, but this type of love is definitely narcissistic. It involves the pursuit of an ideal in order to escape from shame.

Like my client Julia, many Seductive Narcissists are so well defended against shame that they appear extremely poised and self-confident, holding the upper hand in relationships and never at true emotional risk. For others, there's always a danger that shame will break through into awareness. Toward those people who don't hold much psychological value, Seductive Narcissists may consistently come across as self-confident, even arrogant and superior. Toward those people they depend heavily upon to maintain their sense of self, they can seem surprisingly insecure. They may struggle with persistent doubts about their own worth, wanting constantly to hear that they are loved.

Via her carefully constructed persona, Madonna the pop icon appears supremely self-assured. As an entertainer, she exudes a brash self-confidence hostile to social convention and seems always to be saying *Go ahead and disapprove. I don't care what you think.* By contrast, in her personal life (despite the way she exploited her lovers and cast them aside in unfeeling ways) she often comes across as clingy and insecure. She needs continual reassurance from her men that they adore her. When she couldn't identify the whereabouts of one lover, she often telephoned him repeatedly—ten, twenty, thirty times an hour. In tears and desperation, she once refused to begin a concert unless Carlos Leon, her boyfriend of the moment, returned her calls.

While you may find it hard to reconcile such insecurity with her extreme self-confidence, think of them as two halves of the same emotional coin. The ultrapoised, charismatic, "I'm going to rule the world" Madonna embodies a defense against underlying vulnerability. She makes consistent use of other people to shore up her defenses, either by eliciting their admiration when she's in performance mode or demanding reassurance when her fear and need begin to break through. In neither case does the other person exist as a separate being with feelings and needs of his own, but only as a prop to support her fragile sense of self.

Few people have ever gotten close enough to glimpse this vulnerability. Most men and women whose lives have intersected with Madonna's have come away viewing her as unique and superior, destined to distinguish herself. Her high-school drama teacher put it this way: "When the spotlight came on her, she was pure magic. . . . There was no way she could ever be anything other than famous at something. I would watch her on stage with that vibrant personality and charisma, and think to myself, 'Oh, my, it is inevitable, isn't it?'"[15]

At a lower wattage, my client Julia possessed the same quality. So did Harlan, the one-session client I described at the beginning of this chapter. Charisma is a special ability to connect with and influence other people, but it also involves the ability to radiate an impression of elevated personal significance. I don't necessarily mean arrogance or conceit. Charismatic individuals convincingly communicate to the world that they are special or unique, that they have personal qualities and abilities that other people don't possess. While they don't always make other people feel like losers, charismatics definitely come across as the winners in this world. Who doesn't want to be charismatic?

Unlike the Bullying Narcissist, who makes her targets feel like losers, often excluding them from her elite social milieu, the Seductive Narcissist invites spectators to join her in the winner's circle, or at least to stand at the fringe and bask in the reflected glow of her specialness. She makes other people believe that she resides at the center of their particular universe, inspiring them to want contact, to want to emulate her and partake in her superiority. In the 1980s, the term *Madonna wannabe* was coined by writer John Skow to describe young women who took to dressing like the pop star.[16] Many men who met my client Julia wanted to be close to her, to possess her as a way to prove themselves winners. Harlan had an uncanny ability to bend women to his will.

In the political realm, charismatic leaders have a similar effect on the population at large. The philosopher Max Weber first described this phenomenon, defining charisma as a "certain quality of an individual personality, by virtue of which he is set apart from ordinary men and treated as endowed with supernatural, superhuman, or at least specifically exceptional powers or qualities."[17] Cult leaders exert a similar influence upon their followers. For his particular group of adherents, he seems to possess "specially exceptional powers or qualities" that give him an uncanny ability to persuade.

So powerful was his influence over his "family" that Charles Manson convinced them to murder a number of innocent people in brutally cruel ways. In 1978, Jim Jones persuaded over 900 members of his Peoples Temple Agricultural Project, better known as Jonestown, to commit suicide (although evidence exists that some were coerced). David Koresh, the charismatic leader of the Branch Davidian cult in Waco, Texas, led his people on a 51-day stand-off against the FBI and the ATF that eventually led to the death of more than 75 men, women, and children.

It's easy to write off these people (leaders and followers alike) as "crazies," but by thus making them entirely *other*, we lose sight of what we may have in common with them. It's a powerful and widespread human wish to believe that *someone* knows the answers, even if we ourselves do not. We *want* to be led and to have confidence that our leaders know exactly where to take us. For many people, it's beguiling to believe they can simply hand over their doubts and the responsibility for their choices to someone in special communion with the truth, who appears so very certain of what to do.

There seems to be an innate human need to seek out that leader with "specially exceptional powers or qualities." It explains why, election after election, despite what experience has taught us about our past leaders, we so often believe that our preferred candidate is uniquely different and will finally bring about real and lasting change. In many ways, the Seductive Narcissist, the charismatic politician, and the cult leader all succeed in their efforts to wield power over us because, on some level, we're eager to give them that power.

We'll return to this theme in Chapter Seven.

How to Cope with the Seductive Narcissist

Seductive Narcissists pose a special challenge because they often make us feel so good about ourselves that we don't at first recognize them as such. Unlike the Bullying Narcissist, who fills us with a sense of shame and inferiority, the Seductive Narcissist elevates us. He or she makes us feel special, attractive, and eminently desirable, as if we are among the winners in this world. To cope effectively with a Seductive Narcissist, we need to know ourselves very well and have a firm grip on our own narcissistic tendencies.

Few among us can resist the appeal of being adored by someone who makes us feel fascinating and worthwhile. For those of us with parents who fell short in the first of their tasks (that is, to shower us with joyful adoration and to make us feel at the center of their emotional universe), it can be especially difficult to resist the allure of a Seductive Narcissist. We may go through life craving the experience we missed, and when it seems as if we have found it at last, we dive right in. When Seth sent Tina Swithin flowers and bought her that spa package, I'm sure she felt as if she'd won the lottery. And no lottery winner turns down the prize. Not many people in her position would say "I'm not really as special or deserving as you think. We don't even know each other."

Faced with the beguiling charm of a Seductive Narcissist, it's difficult to remain thoughtful and circumspect. Especially in a culture such as ours that idealizes winners and celebrities who appear to have it all, it's hard to resist someone who makes us feel like a rock star. But as Swithin herself remarks, "[I]f things seem too good to be true, they probably are."[18] Idealization has an ugly flip side. "You're perfect" has an unfortunate way of shifting abruptly to "You're worthless." A Seductive Narcissist who makes you feel like a winner can also make you feel like a loser when he's done with you.

At the risk of sounding like a killjoy or a moralistic parent, I offer this advice: The best way to cope with a Seductive Narcissist is to remain modest. Distrust sudden infatuation. Doubt someone who idealizes you before having had time to learn who you really are.

In a larger sense, we need to resist the cultural messaging that divides the world into winners and losers, implying that it's possible to have it all. Most people have been affected by this message to some degree, and the Seductive Narcissist exploits that influence to make you see her as a winner. Remain skeptical of other people who appear "too good to be true." Resist your own urge to idealize as well, especially when you find yourself feeling that life would change dramatically if only you could be close to that other person. It's beguiling to believe that your pain and personal struggles can be resolved by contact with someone who apparently has it all together, who seems to have the answers to everything. It's hard to resist the person who holds out the promise of "happily ever after."

Don't deceive yourself. Perfect happiness doesn't exist, and anyone who seems to suggest otherwise might very well be exploiting you for his own narcissistic ends.

6

"I'M KING OF THE WORLD"
The Grandiose Narcissist

Charismatic leaders project a self-image that inspires confidence. They see themselves as exceptional, a breed apart from ordinary people, and through the power of their conviction, they persuade others to see them in the same light. As a force for good, a healthy kind of narcissism, holding such a self-image reflects a trust in one's strengths and abilities. *I know who I am, I'm sure of what actions to take and confident I can achieve my goals.*

As a destructive force and a type of Extreme Narcissism, the belief that one is exceptional and superior betrays a defensive sense of self out of touch with reality. In order to escape from feelings of core shame—of being small, needy, and defective—the cult leader takes flight from himself and seeks refuge in a grandiose self-image meant to "disprove" all the damage. *I'm not defective. I'm a supremely important person.* It comes as no surprise that Charles Manson, David Koresh, and Jim Jones all emerged from horrific backgrounds.

Manson was born to a fifteen-year-old girl who went to jail for five years when he was only four. Koresh's mother likewise gave birth out of wedlock when she was only fifteen; he never knew his father and was reared largely by his grandparents. Though Jim Jones spent most of his childhood with both parents, his alcoholic father had been disabled by injuries sustained during World War I and the family lived in a shack without plumbing; his mother believed she had given birth to the Messiah. In denial of early trauma and the resulting psychological damage, all three men eventually came to view themselves as exceptional and superior, projecting a grandiose self-image that persuaded others to do their bidding.

These cult leaders appear at the far end of the narcissistic continuum, conforming more or less to the features of Antisocial Personality Disorder, but not all Grandiose Narcissists are so disturbed. Many of them lead relatively stable lives and often accomplish quite a lot by virtue of their conviction that they are exceptional. Many Grandiose Narcissists are drawn to politics, professional sports, and the entertainment industry because success in these fields allows them ample opportunity to demonstrate their winner status and to elicit admiration from others, confirming their defensive self-image as a superior being.

In a culture that reveres celebrity, such Grandiose Narcissists often get off scot free when they behave badly. On camera and before the public eye, they act out their grandiose sense of self—violating social norms, breaking laws, throwing tantrums—with minimal consequences. Fans forgive them and judges go easy. As with the budding narcissist whose parents don't curtail her grandiosity at the appropriate age, the Grandiose Narcissist receives no effective reality check when she displays a lack of respect for other people and no regard for her own limits. Instead, she feels entitled to have and to do whatever she wants.

The behavior of hip-hop recording artist Kanye West provides an especially blatant example. At the 2009 MTV Music Video Awards, in the middle of Taylor Swift's acceptance speech for Best Female Video, West famously rushed the stage, grabbed the microphone from her hand, and proceeded to praise the video he clearly thought should have won—Beyoncé's "Single Ladies." West has a history of bad behavior at awards ceremonies. He walked out of the 2004 American Music Awards after losing the Best New Artist title to country singer Gretchen Wilson. Two years later, he crashed the stage of the 2006 MTV Europe Music Awards and launched into a profanity-laced rant after losing in the Best Hip-Hop Artist category.

His fame and popularity remain undiminished, however. Fans adore him and continue to buy his music: In January 2014, his seventh album went platinum. What reason does he have to reform?

West's over-the-top celebration of his own superiority through his lyrics, interviews, public pronouncements, and misbehaviors has earned him the *narcissist* label from many observers of the cultural scene. His narcissism reflects a grandiosity so profound that he sometimes appears to have lost touch with reality. During a rare interview with the *New York Times*, for example, he proclaimed himself the next Steve Jobs and a major influencer of social trends: "I will be the leader of a company that ends up being worth billions of dollars, because I got the answers. I understand culture. I am the nucleus."[1]

This type of grandiosity often goes hand in hand with a sense of entitlement: *I'm better than other people and not subject to the same rules that apply to them. I have the right to behave in whatever way I choose, regardless of how it affects others, and I should have what I want when I want it.* In their book *The Narcissism Epidemic*, Jean Twenge and W. Keith Campbell argue that inflated self-worth and a sense of entitlement have become pervasive among American youth.[2] A Grandiose Narcissist like Kanye West displays these features in exaggerated form.

West has enough talent and drive to forge a career that validates his inflated self-image to some degree, but many Grandiose Narcissists achieve little, trapped in the world of their dreams and unable or unwilling to do what it takes to make real progress toward a goal.

YOUR NEXT AMERICAN IDOL

I began working with Nicole many years ago when she was referred by a psychiatrist who felt she needed intensive psychotherapy rather than medication. Eighteen years old, angry and depressed, she abused drugs and cut herself with razor blades. She suffered from debilitating insomnia, sleeping no more than a few hours each night. She struggled with gender identity issues and wondered whether she might be a lesbian. Though quite pretty, she did not come across as especially feminine. Something about the way she carried herself—a kind of swagger to her walk and a stiffness in her posture—made her seem a bit mannish.

Nicole came from an intact, middle-class family with a history of mental illness on both sides. Schizophrenic grandfather, a cousin who had committed suicide, more than one case of major depression. From Nicole's description, I gathered that her mother was uncomfortable with affection and prone to brutal sarcasm. Her father came across as jovial, a kind of jokester who appeared warm but was actually quite remote and self-absorbed. She had a jealous older brother who had tortured her throughout childhood.

Even more than the average teen, Nicole felt passionate about rock music. She possessed an encyclopedic knowledge of eminent and obscure musicians. With two of her friends, she went on long road trips to attend concerts in distant cities, following their favorite bands on tour. She revered a number of famous lead singers and indulged fantasies of meeting them, or having sex with them. Most of all, she wanted to be a star herself. Though she had never taken lessons on the guitar and knew only a few rudimentary chords, she saw herself as a megatalent. It was only a matter of time, she believed, before a scout for the record companies would sign her up and make her a star.

Nicole composed many songs and sometimes played them for me during our sessions—simple pop tunes demonstrating an ear for catchy melodies, but they were ultimately boring, without much complexity. She had no background in composition, nor had she ever played with other musicians in a band. She frequently told me, with obvious pride, that she had perfect pitch. Whenever she brought her tape recorder to a session and played songs for me, she obviously expected me to be overcome with admiration.

Though Nicole viewed herself as a "secret genius" destined for greatness, she had no idea how to develop as a musician. She often talked of forming a band but never did so. On occasion, it occurred to her that she should take lessons, and she eventually did find a teacher. She studied with him for only a few months because the difficulty of practicing and the slow pace of the progress she made enraged her. She believed she shouldn't have to work at it: A musical genius would simply *know* how to play.

A year or so into her treatment, Nicole's parents refused to continue paying for her sessions. By that point, I had already reduced my fee substantially so that she could come several times per week. Given the severity of her difficulties and especially my concerns about self-injury, I knew I needed to see her that often. When Nicole informed me that her parents would no longer pay, she asked, "What am I going to do now?" She sounded both angry and afraid. She knew she needed her sessions.

"I guess you'll have to get a job and pay for them yourself."

My answer infuriated Nicole. She expected me to see her for free; the very idea that she would now have to take financial responsibility for herself struck her as an outrage.

We had a number of difficult sessions about the issue, some of them cut short when Nicole stormed out of my office, slamming the door behind her. She always came back. Despite the enraged sense of entitlement, she understood on some level that I cared about her and was trying to help her find her way. Eventually, she began looking for work. At first, she earned money posing nude for art classes and imagined that she might become a highly successful runway model. She enjoyed having the artists in class look at her. Maybe one of them would tell an agent-friend about this great beauty he had discovered.

Nicole later found a job in retail and managed to keep it, despite the anger she felt about having to work at a job she considered beneath her. During this time, our sessions focused on her rage and sense of entitlement. She insisted that I should be willing to work for free and that someone else should be paying the rest of her bills. She should have become a rock star by now, living an opulent, privileged life. I made many interpretations about her hatred of reality—the long, hard work involved in achieving anything of value in the real world. I often said, "You feel you should just have what you want when you want it." I talked about running from the experience of being small and helpless, becoming big all at once—a rock star, a top model, a musical genius.

In those days, I hadn't yet evolved the views about core shame that I currently hold. Today, I might say to Nicole something different, something like this: "You're afraid you're so messed up inside that there's no hope of getting better. You're afraid you're so damaged that it's pointless even to try. The only way out seems to be by magic, to suddenly change into somebody completely different—a winner 'you' who has it all." I would have spoken with feeling about the agony of shame, too, and hopefully made her feel that I empathized with the depth of her suffering.

The original interpretations I did make to Nicole weren't incorrect. They reflect a different but compatible perspective on the emotional issues involved. Yes, Nicole struggled with feeling small, needy, and helpless, but that experience also fueled her profound sense of shame and a fear that she was damaged beyond repair. The Grandiose Narcissist experiences need as shameful and equates neediness with being a loser. She takes refuge in a fantasy of having it all. In other words, the Grandiose Narcissist rejects and disowns her needy loser self, taking refuge in a fantasized image of herself as a winner.

Over time, Nicole learned to tolerate feeling small and inexperienced, to endure the frustration involved in persistent work over time rather than taking grandiose flight. Within the context of a psychotherapy relationship in which she felt seen, understood, and accepted, she eventually faced the underlying shame about her psychological damage, even if we didn't use that particular word in those days.

Nicole eventually enrolled in college and chose a profession. She found a new guitar teacher and, after a number of years, became quite proficient at it. She studied composition and put her talents to good use, writing more complex and musically satisfying songs. Though she didn't pursue a career in music, she formed a band with friends and occasionally played small clubs in the city where they lived. Mostly, they played together for their enjoyment.

Based on some recent studies that attempt to assess how narcissists unconsciously feel about themselves, Twenge and Campbell argue that narcissism is *not* a cover for insecurity and low self-esteem (a commonly held belief) and that even on an unconscious level narcissists harbor an image of themselves as superior to others.[3] But Brad J. Bushman and Roy F. Baumeister refine this view to distinguish between *stable* and *unstable* types of self-esteem: Individuals who react with hostility and defensiveness to narcissistic injuries typically have an unstable self-image that is highly dependent upon support and reinforcement from the outside.[4] This instability, I would argue, reflects the *defensive* nature of the person's self-image; doubts about its validity are a constant threat.

In other words, for the Extreme Narcissist engaged in the *relentless narcissistic defense* (Chapter Three), each challenge to his self-esteem threatens an outbreak of core shame.

If I introduce the idea of core shame too early in therapy with clients like Nicole, they will usually reject it or feel attacked, though they may bring in dreams that symbolically reflect a sense of pervasive inner damage. Wrecked or burned-out cars, squalid tenement buildings and rundown shacks, a landscape decimated by nuclear war—these are some of the dream images I have encountered that reflect the experience of core shame. Sometimes there will be a deformed or diseased baby, or one suffering from extreme neglect, festering in dirty diapers, riddled with disease. The dreamer usually doesn't appear in her own dream; rather, these images of damage, disease, and decay symbolize her experience of a self in ruins.

Early in our work, Nicole brought in a simple dream image that shed light on her sense of self. She herself doesn't appear in the dream. Rather, a scientist with large black glasses stands onstage behind a podium. He sports a white lab coat, with a mortarboard on his head. Underneath his lab coat, he is wearing diapers that need to be changed. The image reminded Nicole of Mr. Peabody, a character from a favorite childhood cartoon, "Peabody's Improbable History." In this cartoon, Mr. Peabody is a beagle who happens to be the smartest being in existence and has accomplished incredible things in life as a business magnate, inventor, Nobel laureate, two-time Olympic medalist, et cetera.[5] Nicole's dream conveyed the sense of a grandiose but fraudulent self, a baby masquerading as a highly accomplished scientist of note.

Nicole's parents failed in the first of their tasks, to instill in their daughter a sense of her beauty and goodness, to make her feel at the center of her universe. As our work progressed, it became clear that her mother had probably suffered from postpartum depression and failed to bond with her baby. In her earliest visual memories from childhood, Nicole "saw" her mother reading romance novels on the couch, off in her own fictional world. She also recalled crawling around in the backyard, alone, and finding dog excrement on the lawn. Whether this memory was authentic, it reflected the experience of neglect and isolation. It was "true" in a psychological sense.

Parents who fail in the second of their tasks (to curtail their child's grandiosity at the appropriate age) may also produce a Grandiose Narcissist. In their analysis of current parenting styles and the self-esteem movement, Twenge and Campbell show how even well-intentioned and relatively healthy parents encourage narcissism in their children, but Narcissistic Parents who escape from their own shame by living vicariously through their children have an especially pernicious influence. Like Earl Woods, they may idealize their children to such a degree that their son or daughter never learns humility and a regard for the feelings of others. Because these boys and girls are usually spoiled and constantly praised, regardless of how well they do, they may grow up feeling entitled to have what they want without doing the work to earn it.

LACKING FOR NOTHING

During her pregnancy, Anne and her husband, John, spent hours scouring baby-name books because they wanted their child to have a very special name. Anne had always disliked her own name, originally spelled without the final *e*, which she had added during college to make it seem more genteel, more English—after Anne Elliot from Jane Austen's novel *Persuasion*. John had come from a long family line of Johns, most of them alcoholics, all of them *losers* as far as he was concerned. Anne and John wanted their child to have a name that would set him or her apart from other children.

After the ultrasound showed that Anne was carrying a boy, they finally settled on *Shiloh*. Even before he was born, Anne and John did everything they could to ensure that their child would be a success in life. Although she had never cared much for classical music, Anne put Mozart on the stereo while Shiloh was still in utero because she'd read somewhere that classical music stimulated fetal brain development. After he was born, they hung a mobile with soft block letters over his crib and continually recited the alphabet to him. They read to him every night, of course.

Whenever Anne's divorced mother came to visit her grandson, which fortunately wasn't very often, she offered no help but lots of unwanted advice. "You're going to spoil that child," she often said. "Just because he whines that way doesn't mean you have to drop everything and go running." Anne had never felt close to her mother and was always relieved to see her go. John had long ago broken off all contact with his own family.

As he grew older, Shiloh did not disappoint, at least not during elementary school. At parent-teacher conferences, he was usually described as "very bright" and "a hard worker," though more than one teacher remarked that he had trouble taking criticism. "We believe praise does a lot more good than criticism," Anne would explain. On occasion, he would come home from school in a foul mood after receiving only a B on a test. Anne and John gave nonstop encouragement, applauding all his schoolwork no matter how shoddy or incomplete, regardless of the grade he received. They told him nearly every day that he was special. According to the child-rearing books Anne had read, it was important for parents to build a child's self-esteem with such praise.

Troubles began to surface in middle school, when Shiloh was caught cheating on a math test. After hearing from the principal, Anne and John sat down with Shiloh to discuss why cheating was wrong. Shiloh seemed indifferent. "Everybody cheats," he said. In his most forceful voice (which wasn't terribly authoritative), John told him, "Don't let it happen again." After careful thought, Anne and

John decided to take away Shiloh's iPad for two weeks—an entirely ineffective punishment, since he simply shifted over to his laptop and spent more time playing video games on his PlayStation.

In high school, Shiloh's grades began to drop. When his parents exhorted him to work harder, he complained that school was boring. When they asked, "How do you expect to get into a good college?" he only shrugged. They tried offering financial rewards for better grades, but this had no effect. He always seemed to have enough money to support his social life, and Anne sometimes wondered how he could go so often to rock concerts and out to dinner with friends on the allowance they gave him. She suspected he was taking money from her billfold and began concealing it in her bedroom, but she never confronted him directly.

For his sixteenth birthday, John and Anne bought Shiloh a new Honda Civic, for which he thanked them without much enthusiasm. He later remarked that his best friend, Isaac, drove a BMW, making clear that he thought a Honda beneath him. As his grades sank even lower, Anne began searching his room and finally discovered a few joints concealed inside a pair of rolled-up socks. They grounded Shiloh and took away the keys to his car for a month; he then slipped out his bedroom window late at night, walked a block or so down the street, and was picked up by friends. Though she never discussed it with her husband, Anne knew what Shiloh was doing but feared he might turn against them if they cracked down any harder.

Shiloh was a good-looking boy who had no trouble getting dates, though he never saw any girl for long. His parents couldn't keep track of all their names—practically a new one every few weeks. From the arrogant way he talked and the dismissive way he referred to these girls, Anne worried that he saw himself as "God's gift to women."

Though he didn't come out and say so, John saw Shiloh as a "player" and took secret pride in his son's exploits. Until he met Anne, John had never experienced much success with girls and had considered himself a romantic flop.

After they caught Shiloh and his current girl in bed (she had snuck in through the bedroom window), John and Anne quarreled over how to punish him. "He's a teenage boy," John argued. "He's got raging hormones." When the girl's irate father called, complaining that Shiloh had texted explicit photos of his daughter to friends, John finally conceded that Anne might be right and they took away his car keys one more time.

Despite high SAT scores, Shiloh's poor grades shut him out of the best schools and he wound up at the local community college. He dropped out after two semesters, complaining of boredom. "Why should I go through four years of stupid pointless classes, just so I can get some crappy job?" He seemed to have no ambition, though at the same time, he felt entitled to the benefits of hard work. Anne noticed one day that some of her jewelry was missing from the box on her dresser. Shiloh denied taking it but couldn't explain how he had paid for his new leather jacket. She didn't press the point.

John and Anne couldn't understand why Shiloh needed to fill up his car's gas tank so often—they'd given him an Exxon card to be used exclusively for gas—and finally realized that he was filling up his friends' cars, too, and taking their cash. When they canceled the card, Shiloh called them "fucking misers" and moved out. After that, he worked at a long series of low-level jobs but could never hold them down. Either he quit because he found the job tedious or his employer would fire him for insolence. Every few years, he'd call his parents in financial extremis; time after time, they would bail him out.

*　　*　　*

You may have known someone like Shiloh who, despite innate gifts and supportive parents, can't seem to get started in adult life. With the best of intentions, parents like Anne and John foster an attitude of entitlement in their children. Often in flight from their own families of origin, they understandably try to give their sons and daughters what they themselves lacked growing up. When driven by core shame, they may also want their children to become winners who will redeem their own lives. In the face of permissive parenting, too much uncritical praise, and ineffective punishments, boys and girls like Shiloh grow up feeling that they are exceptional, not subject to the usual rules, and entitled to the best of everything without having to work for it.

Like my client Nicole at the beginning of our work together, these individuals can't set realistic goals and sustain the effort necessary to achieve them. In contrast to many of the Extreme Narcissists you've met in these pages, their narcissism may sometimes be difficult to detect because they live out their grandiose self-image in quiet fantasy, retreating from the demands and limitations of the real world. Like Nicole, they may feel themselves to be secret geniuses misunderstood by everyone they know. Sometimes they hatch get-rich-quick schemes, briefly pursue them with great energy, and then give up.

A culture that reveres celebrity, deluging us with images of actors and rock stars who appear to "have it all," also tends to encourage unhealthy narcissism in growing children. Especially when they see famous people behaving outrageously in public and suffering no consequences as a result, they may come to feel that celebrities truly are special, not subject to the usual rules, and then try to emulate them.

"I'm King of the World": The Grandiose Narcissist

As Drew Pinsky and S. Mark Young note in their book about the influence of celebrity narcissism on American youth, for those who suffered from childhood trauma, this effect is especially toxic.[6] Nicole longed to escape from core shame; the revered cultural icon of rock star seemed to point the way out.

The cult of celebrity also harms people like Shiloh, young men and women whose childhood was not marred by trauma but who grew up in a world where being rich and famous is viewed as the highest good. Especially when combined with permissive parenting, where children are reared to become social winners in order to redeem their parents' unconscious shame, an atmosphere of celebrity worship encourages their narcissistic tendencies.

You may be familiar with a famous survey conducted several years ago, in which 650 teenagers in Rochester were asked about their personal ambitions as well as their views on fame. The result that made headlines found that 43.4 percent of these children aspired to be "the personal assistant to a very famous singer or movie star," whereas only 23.7 percent would have liked to be "the president of a great university like Harvard or Yale."[7] An academic job probably doesn't sound all that interesting to your average fifteen-year-old, but it's nonetheless striking that this group values *mere affiliation* with a celebrity over their own accomplishments in some other arena.

Another result of this survey, which received less press, found that teenagers who described themselves as lonely and frequently depressed were more likely than their peers to believe that becoming a celebrity would lead to happiness. As a result of an emotionally chaotic or traumatic family life, these children see celebrity as the answer to their problems, an escape from core shame. The more socially isolated kids believe that becoming famous would win them friends: They would become social winners, rather than the outcast losers they feel themselves to be.

STANDING UP FOR THE LITTLE MAN

While movie stars or pop singers don't usually achieve their fame because they embody higher social values (they are often "famous for being famous," in the well-known description of social historian Daniel Boorstin),[8] several celebrities in recent years have become cultural heroes because they *appeared* to be the very antithesis of the shallow celebrity narcissist. Apparently virtuous or selfless men, in the end they turned out to be Extreme Narcissists manipulating their public image for glory and financial gain.

Lance Armstrong persuaded his fans that he was a man of almost superhuman virtue—a tireless competitor who would never ever cheat, a courageous cancer survivor and all-around good guy. In *Three Cups of Tea*, Greg Mortenson portrays himself as a preternaturally selfless man, a monklike crusader for the educational rights of young girls in Afghanistan. Both men turned out to be masters of cultivating public perception. Although their charitable foundations, LiveStrong and the Central Asia Institute, did much good, a closer look at the psychology of these men reveals the features of Extreme Narcissism and points toward core shame.[9]

Julian Assange, founder of WikiLeaks and tireless crusader against the secrecy of entrenched power, for a time appeared to be another hero in our feckless world. Standing up for truth, transparency, and the rights of the individual to access secret government information, Assange at first seemed to be a selfless advocate for the little man. He turned out to be a Grandiose Narcissist more interested in public acclaim and enjoying his "rock star" status than in pursuing the truth.

Ghostwriter Andrew O'Hagan spent many months collaborating with Julian Assange on an autobiography and in the process came to know him well. "His pursuit of governments and corporations was a ghostly reverse of his own fears for himself," O'Hagan writes. "That was the big secret with him: he wanted to cover up everything about himself except his fame. . . . The man who put himself in charge of disclosing the world's secrets simply couldn't bear his own."

In the end, O'Hagan concluded, it may turn out that Assange "was motivated all the while not by high principles but by a deep sentimental wound." He doesn't specify the exact nature of that "sentimental wound," but he clearly links it to Assange's childhood.[10]

In a profile appearing in the *New Yorker*, Assange describes his early childhood as "pretty Tom Sawyer. . . . I had my own horse. I built my own raft. I went fishing. I was going down mine shafts and tunnels."[11] Assange portrays himself as an intensely independent and curious youth, an intrepid hero in the making. He may actually have owned his own horse and explored secret underground passageways, but this account conceals a childhood marked by chaos. Assange's mother, Christine, met and fell in love with John Shipton when she was only seventeen; not long after Julian was born, Shipton disappeared from their lives and didn't see his son for another twenty-five years.

When Julian was one, Christine married theater director Brett Assange, and they collaborated on various productions, moving frequently around Australia. According to Andrew O'Hagan, Assange told him during their collaboration that his stepfather had been an alcoholic, though he later tried to suppress this disclosure.[12] When Julian was eight, Christine left her husband, took up with a "musician," and soon gave birth to another child, a son. The relationship was "tempestuous," the musician turned abusive, and they eventually separated.

During a legal battle over custody of Assange's half-brother, Christine took flight with her two children, fearing that the musician would try to take her son away. In numerous interviews, including recorded conversations with O'Hagan, Assange has stated that the musician belonged to a powerful New Age cult called the Family, whose motto was "Unseen, Unknown, and Unheard." Although his mother later insisted that the idea of cult membership was purely "speculative" and wasn't even discussed until her son was a teenager, Assange tells a different story. According to his version, mother and children lived on the run from the time Julian was eleven until he turned sixteen, in constant fear of the cult and its power. Depending on which interview you read, Assange had attended between twelve and thirty-seven schools by the time he turned fourteen. He has also said that he lived in either thirty or fifty different towns while growing up.

None of this sounds particularly carefree or adventurous. Despite the Tom Sawyer spin, Assange's childhood in fact resembles the early family life of other figures profiled in this book, in particular that of Lance Armstrong: abandonment by his biological father, a problematic relationship with a stepfather, an atmosphere at home that turned emotionally abusive. The account of persecution by a nefarious cult may be largely fictional, an early sign of his tendency to find enemies who enhance his own self-importance, but this hardly sounds like a happy childhood.

Like Armstrong, Assange found a way out, his own chance to "become something." During his teens, he developed a passionate interest in computers and programming. Working under the moniker

Mendax (which roughly translates as "nobly untruthful," from Horace's *splendide mendax*), he earned a reputation within the international hacking subculture as a "sophisticated programmer who could break into the most secure networks." He later joined with two other hackers to form the International Subversives, a virtual collective that broke into computer systems in Australia, Europe, and North America, including networks that belonged to the U.S. Department of Defense and to the Los Alamos National Laboratory.

He found the experience of his own power intoxicating:

> It was certainly addictive. You'd dive down into a computer system—typically, for me at the time, the Pentagon's 8th Command Group computers. You'd take it over, projecting your mind all the way from your untidy bedroom to the entire system along the halls, and all the while you're learning to understand that system better than the people in Washington. It was like being able to teleport yourself into the interior of the Pentagon in order to walk around and take charge.[13]

A self-aware sort of grandiosity permeates his words: Assange acknowledges the druglike thrill of escaping that "untidy bedroom" for the virtual corridors of power. He feels superior in understanding to those in Washington who are responsible for the computer system he has hijacked. He enjoys the experience of thumbing his nose at authority and taking charge himself.

With the founding of WikiLeaks, Assange found an even larger stage upon which to express his grandiose sense of self. He surely felt a passionate devotion to his cause—uncovering the government lies that preserve its power over the individual—but as the enterprise gained notoriety and he became a cult hero to millions, he increasingly saw himself as a sort of celebrity guru, often insisting that one person or another was in love with him, or wanted to *be* him. In his account of their years together at WikiLeaks, Daniel Domscheit-Berg paints a portrait of Assange as a man obsessed with his image, unwilling to share credit with collaborators, hostile to those who didn't accord him due respect, and contemptuous of even those who supported him.[14] He treated his collaborators as if they were his subjects.

Assange's grandiosity had an increasingly paranoid flavor. He identified with historical figures who had been persecuted, such as Alexander Solzhenitsyn, the Russian dissident, or even Jesus Christ. One of his favorite activities was to scour the Internet for references to himself, especially by his detractors, and he seemed to have an "unending capacity to worry about his enemies."[15] Even before the founder of WikiLeaks became famous, he often insisted that government agents were trailing him or eavesdropping on his phone calls.

Once the Afghanistan War logs were released and he may actually have been trailed, Assange routinely demanded that followers search the bushes for "assassins" before he would emerge from the car. He told taxi drivers to pull onto side streets because he believed he was being followed. And he "appeared to like the notion that he was being pursued," viewing himself as the hero of a Cold War era thriller, constantly threatened by nefarious villains concealed within the shadows. Bill Keller, editor of the *New York Times*, eventually came to see Assange as "a character from a Stieg Larsson thriller."

Assange also had a habit of alienating friends and turning collaborators into adversaries. Not long after the Afghanistan War logs were released, he fell out with journalists and editors at the *Guardian*, insisting that they had "double-crossed" him and accusing them of cowardice. He likewise turned against his former collaborators at the *New York Times* and *Der Spiegel*. When the *Times* decided not to link their coverage to the WikiLeaks website, based on concerns that the names of informants had not been properly redacted (concerns that turned out to have been well founded), Assange telephoned Bill Keller and demanded, "Where's the respect?" Keller subsequently wrote a long piece for the magazine describing Assange as brilliant and highly skilled but also arrogant, paranoid, and thin skinned.[16]

For a Grandiose Narcissist like Assange who eventually achieves fame or notoriety, real-life experience confirms an inflated self-image that predates his success. The fact that he became Public Enemy No. 1 to a superpower helped bolster long-standing psychological defenses against core shame—that "sentimental wound" about which O'Hagan has speculated. It's as if Assange went searching for enemies; feeling persecuted and betrayed made him feel like a martyr, linking him in his own mind to important historical figures who had suffered a similar fate. Even if he sometimes had good reason to fear his adversaries, his paranoia reflects a defensive and grandiose self-image meant to ward off shame.

How to Cope with the Grandiose Narcissist

No matter how many times our heroes fall from their pedestals, filling us with disillusionment, it seems we continue searching for new ones to replace them. Human beings apparently have an innate need for leaders or role models they can look up to and aspire to emulate. The Grandiose Narcissist who appears to embody our ideals, often by manipulating his public persona, plays into that need by presenting himself as a hero, and by nature, we are easily seduced.

As with the Seductive Narcissist, resisting manipulation depends upon a healthy skepticism concerning human nature: If he seems too good to be true—saint or superhero in the midst of us mortals—he probably is. Because the Grandiose Narcissist may crusade on behalf of causes we actually believe in—promoting education for poor Muslim girls, for example, or challenging entrenched power—he uses our admiration to exploit us. We *want* to believe in him. He may appear to be an altruistic agent in the service of a worthy cause, but his motivations are quite selfish.

How many people do you know who are truly selfless?

Within our more immediate world, the Grandiose Narcissist may show up in a leadership position, at work or in our social lives, frequently armed with charisma. Due to the persuasive power of their self-image, these people may be difficult to resist. We find ourselves wanting to associate with these winners, as if their superiority will rub off on us and make us winners, too. In other words, the Grandiose Narcissist exploits our own tendency to view the world in terms of winners and losers. Although we don't consciously realize it, we might fear that resisting the call and challenging their grandiosity will exclude us from the winner's circle.

Do you long to be a winner, associating with other members of the elite?

A Grandiose Narcissist like Nicole poses no such threat because she lives out her inflated self-image in the realm of fantasy; we immediately recognize that she is self-deceived. Though his parents supported his sense of entitlement, most people would find an underachiever like Shiloh easy to rebuff when he asked for money. In short, the Grandiose Narcissist who disengages from the world because it doesn't support his inflated self-image is easy to resist, but the one who "confirms" his grandiosity through actual achievements can deceive us, especially when we share his winner-loser mindset.

7

"I HAVE SO MUCH TO TELL YOU"
The Know-It-All Narcissist

Several years ago, I attended an awards banquet for one of my children, where I was seated at a table with other parents. I knew several of those parents fairly well but I also met a new couple, Chet and Monica, who had a daughter in my son's grade. Chet worked in commercial banking and Monica headed up the human resources department of a major corporation. With her long painted nails and hair parted down the middle, neatly curving around her cheeks, Monica reminded me of Barbra Streisand back in the 1970s. She had a habit of using those long nails to claw back strands of hair when they slipped forward onto her face.

Monica talked more or less continuously in the lead-up to the awards ceremony. She didn't seem anxious, and given that she was a human resources expert, I assumed she must be comfortable speaking with people she didn't know well. At the same time, for a person whose job involved getting to know employees in order to address their workplace difficulties, she seemed entirely unfamiliar with the process of asking questions. In fact, she showed no interest whatsoever in the other parents at the table, though she talked *at* us at great length, without pausing to draw breath.

"I love that shirt!" she told me not long after I took my seat. "My husband has one a lot like it in his closet back home. You know, now that I look at it, I think it may actually be the very same one. He bought it when we were in the Bahamas. Now *that* was an amazing trip!" Thereafter followed a long tale about shopping for emeralds in Nassau, with frequent mention of the extravagant prices Monica paid and lots of bemused comments about the number of piña coladas she drank. She laughed loudly at her own story though it wasn't terribly funny.

If any of us tried to change the subject, Monica swiftly found a way to redirect each detour back in her own direction. "So your younger daughter goes to Estes Hills Elementary? We have good friends who just bought a house in that area. I was actually the one who found them the house, because I always keep a close eye on the real estate market around town. I've helped a lot of my friends find houses. I guess you could call me a sort of real estate matchmaker." She laughed. I gave a knowing look to one of the other parents at the table, a well-respected real estate broker who had worked in our area for years.

As it turned out, Monica also knew an awful lot about a great many things other than real estate, and she generously shared her knowledge with those of us trapped around the banquet table that evening. Based largely on her experience watching *Mad Men*, she seemed to know more about advertising than anyone else, including a man who'd spent much of his career producing TV commercials at big ad agencies in New York. She knew even more about our school district than the man seated at my right, who held a seat on the school board. The extent of Monica's knowledge was truly formidable.

You've undoubtedly met people like Monica, at parties or possibly at your place of work. Maybe someone in your social circle or even your family is this kind of Know-It-All Narcissist, forever demonstrating her superior understanding, always ready to share her wisdom and give you unwanted advice. Sometimes such people are merely boring and self-impressed, but when they completely dominate a social event like that banquet I attended, they become offensive.

Know-It-All Narcissists, though not as extreme as some of the other narcissists you'll meet in this book, can nonetheless be a destructive force in your world. And while you might view them as nothing but social bores, caught up in their own stories and oblivious to other people, they actually exploit us in much the same way that other Extreme Narcissists do. Monica needed an audience of people to bear witness to her superior knowledge and insight. She wanted us to see her as a winner. At the same time, because she understood the ways of the world so much better than the rest of us, she turned us into comparative losers, people who knew far less than she did. In other words, like all Extreme Narcissists, the Know-It-All Narcissist supports an inflated sense of self—*at our expense.*

As children, these individuals often excelled academically; they may have appeared intellectually precocious and were rewarded for it by their families. Knowing more than their classmates and getting better grades offered relief from shame, for the child and sometimes for the parents, too, who may have taken narcissistic pride in having such a gifted child. Precocity gives children a way to "disprove" their fears of being damaged, small, and inferior. Nicole's dream from the last chapter—the brilliant scientist with dirty diapers concealed beneath his lab coat—depicts such precocity and what lies behind it.

No doubt you remember a Know-It-All Narcissist from your own schooling. He was the boy who always had his hand up, the one who made other students sigh or roll their eyes when he started to speak.

Oh no! There he goes again.

As adults, these men and women make difficult colleagues in the workplace. Like Monica, they tend to monopolize conversations, reject input from their co-workers, and have a "my way or the highway" attitude toward decision-making. Because they're usually thinking ahead to what they want to say next, they don't listen to potentially useful input from other people. They may come across as brusque, aggressive, or even contemptuous, dismissing other viewpoints out of hand in ways that alienate their colleagues. The Know-It-All Narcissist makes a poor team member and always wants to lead.

Not every Know-It-All Narcissist is as blatant as Monica. Many of them find more subtle ways to demonstrate superior knowledge, with casual asides slipped into conversation. And "knowing it all" doesn't always depend upon having facts at hand. It can mean privileged access to powerful or important people, as if such familiarity makes the insider special and gives his opinions greater weight than yours. It can mean a more intimate knowledge of foreign countries, proving that he's worldlier and more experienced than you. It can reflect a deeper knowledge of books, music, movies, or even TV shows, as if he's *au courant* and you are not.

"I Have So Much to Tell You": The Know-It-All Narcissist

This type of Know-It-All Narcissist might be a name-dropper, peppering conversation with references to eminent or influential people you don't personally know. She might make casual mention of the exotic places she has visited where you've never been, or allude to parties she attended (to which you obviously weren't invited). She might talk about her visit to the latest trendy restaurant or club, insisting that you go there on her recommendation. As a result, the Know-It-All Narcissist often comes across as a snob. Whether it's blatant or subtle, she always tries to raise herself above others, to prove that her exclusive familiarity with people, places, or trends makes her superior to her audience.

When people try so hard to demonstrate their superiority, they usually feel quite differently about themselves on another level and want to keep that feeling hidden. The word *pretentious* conveys the idea of disguise: It means that the person pretends to be *more*, in one way or another, than he truly is. By now it should come as no surprise that the Know-It-All Narcissist often struggles with core shame—the unconscious sense of defect, inferiority, or ugliness. Men and women like Monica so relentlessly enforce their defensive identity that their shame remains entirely hidden, from themselves as well as from other people, but if you ever get to know them well, you often find lurking insecurities and self-doubt.

"I AM NOTHING LIKE THEM"

Jesse came to me during his freshman year in college because of persistent depression that had begun to affect his grades. As a precocious child, he'd always done well academically, and he graduated from high school at the top of his class, without ever having to put in much effort. As a result, he lacked self-discipline and found the demands of college work more challenging than he had anticipated. At the time therapy began, he was also struggling with his sexuality and the growing awareness that his deepest attractions were to men.

Jesse worried that he might seem effeminate but he came across as *affected* more than anything else, due to his slightly condescending air. He often spoke in dismissive ways of people he found ignorant or uncultured, and he had a set of pet peeves concerning common gram-matical errors. During one session, for example, he told me he was "shocked" that one of his professors had actually said "that's a whole 'nother story." It bothered him that so many people misused the word *aggravate* to express annoyance when it actually means "to intensify or make worse." He took pride in speaking correctly and at times could seem pretentious.

Though he had never been to Great Britain, he was a devoted Anglophile, with ideas about the English culled largely from Victo-rian novels and programs on public television such as *Downton Abbey*. Jesse felt he had been born in the wrong era, the wrong country, and the wrong class. During high school, he had begun to study French and continued during his first year in college. He regarded the abil-ity to speak that language as a sign of sophistication. He also made a point of pronouncing French words imported into English with the correct native accent: *rendezvous, hors d'oeuvre, amateur,* et cetera.

As his therapist, I at first found it a challenge to empathize with Jesse because he often treated me with a superior, condescending manner. Early in our work, Jesse would occasionally express a dis-dainful opinion in a way that assumed I would agree with him, but more often he treated me with mild contempt, as if I were ignorant or inferior. In other words, he treated me as a carrier for the shame he had disavowed. When a client's defenses against unconscious shame so dominate his personality, it can be difficult to connect emotionally with his pain.

Though he came from an intact family that appeared relatively normal from the outside, Jesse's parents were both alcoholics. He had virtually no relationship with his father, who worked long hours and drank hard at home. He described his mother as depressed, with a blunt, sarcastic sense of humor that she inflicted upon everyone else in the family. Jesse's older brother had sold drugs as a teenager and eventually dropped out of high school, left home at the age of seventeen, and moved to another state. His younger sister was still in high school, painfully shy and suffering from an eating disorder.

Jesse told me that he had always felt like an outsider in his family because of his intellectual and cultural interests. Unlike his parents and siblings, he was a voracious reader and passionate about the performing arts, from classical music to the theater. Though unable to buy alcohol legally, he could tell you the names of all the grapes typically found in a wine from Bordeaux and knew the best vintages. His parents, by contrast, placed large bottles of jug wine on the table at dinner each night. I had the sense that emphasizing his differences allowed him to set himself apart from the family's dysfunction, as if to say *They're a bunch of ignorant, fucked-up losers and I am nothing like them.*

Jesse was a prolific dreamer and regularly brought in dreams of the type I describe in Chapter Six, the sense of a self-in-ruins portrayed through images of derelict cars and rundown shacks. From time to time, he would also report dreaming that he was trapped in the basement of a building with broken sewer lines. Water full of feces and urine would spew from the pipes, filling the room and rising above his ankles. In those dreams, Jesse would recognize that he had to find some way to stop the flow of sewage but felt helpless to do anything about it. He often startled awake with a feeling of terror, his body and sheets soaked in sweat.

In working with dream symbolism, I have often found that raw sewage represents a client's unacknowledged emotional experience—all the unconscious feelings (down there in the "basement") too painful to be faced. Relying on different defense mechanisms, the client may have successfully repressed awareness of his pain, but on another level, he feels as if it is "backing up"; like Jesse, he may fear the psychic pressure will keep building and eventually break through into awareness, flooding him with unbearable pain. Raw sewage conveys the idea of unprocessed experience, emotions so agonizing that they can't be thought about or understood and only evacuated.

For Jesse, these dreams also reflected his fear that he would be exposed as a fraud, a "piece of shit" passing himself off as a worldly sophisticate. Nicole's dream of the diaper-wearing scientist conveyed a similar idea of imposture. In order to escape the unbearable experience of a defective, shame-ridden, and "shitty" self, the precocious child constructs a new superior self to conceal and deny all the damage. Though he may come across as snobby, condescending, or contemptuous, he fears exposure as a fraud. He appears to believe that he knows it all, but he fears that he actually knows nothing of real worth.

Over the course of several years, Jesse gradually let go of his pretensions and allowed me to see his true self. In the process, I came to feel a deep affection for him as he stopped using me as a carrier for his unconscious experience. More and more, he learned to bear with and explore (rather than defend against) his shame. He also came to accept his sexuality. His relationships improved as he descended to earth and let other people get to know the real Jesse.

THE NARCISSIST GURU

The Know-It-All Narcissist doesn't always come across as self-important or pretentious. Especially if he happens to be a charismatic individual, he may instead convince his audience that he actually does possess special knowledge that makes him superior. Religious or spiritual leaders, physicians, and teachers may at first appear to be reliable guides rather than narcissists. In my own profession, I've also known several extremely self-assured, charismatic therapists who give the impression of having the inside track on truth. For those who are lost or confused and in search of professional help, such therapists exert a magnetic appeal. Who doesn't want to believe his or her therapist has the answers?

The narcissistic therapist sometimes achieves gurulike status. His clients and the therapists-in-training whom he supervises may come to revere or idealize him; he feeds off their adoration, exploiting it to sustain his grandiose self-image as enlightened healer. It's not so unusual for clients to believe they have "the best therapist in the world," but the narcissistic therapist subtly encourages this belief. His junior colleagues may see him as one of the very few people who truly understand how to practice psychotherapy, devoting years of their lives and tens of thousands of dollars to private supervision. There are predatory therapists who deliberately prey upon those in their care, exploiting them sexually and financially. They pursue their own desires with a ruthless disregard for other people's feelings.

Such individuals occupy the very far end of the narcissistic continuum and are best described as sociopaths. But the Know-It-All Narcissist who becomes a therapist doesn't see herself as exploitative. She usually believes that she truly cares for her clients. She feels good about herself because she's able to help so many people whom only she can reach.

We all want to believe that the work we do is valued by others, of course, but as a therapist, the Know-It-All Narcissist needs to feel she has *much, much more* to offer than anyone else in her profession. While she may come across as a saint to her clients and those she supervises, she is hypercompetitive with her peers and privately contemptuous of them. Dr. T, a narcissistic therapist I know, once sat on a panel with a visiting professional who had an international reputation and greater professional standing; Dr. T delivered a critique of the man's ideas so savage that it reduced him to tears.

In the privacy of her consulting room, the narcissistic therapist can be quite seductive. She might imply or even directly state that she has a "special" relationship with you. Through her personal disclosures, she makes you feel privileged to have such access to her private life. Perhaps she gives you extra time at the end of your session—evidence of her deep concern for you. If she also gives you praise, telling you how insightful you are and how well you seem to understand and appreciate her work, you might feel part of an elite duo. Like the Seductive Narcissist, she makes you feel good about yourself so you'll admire her in return.

Not surprisingly, the narcissistic therapist has trouble acknowledging mistakes and insists upon her own omniscience. If you find fault with her, rather than admitting error, she may blame you instead. Or she may become hurt, angry, or contemptuous if you confront her.

She might take a "my way or the highway" approach to treatment, insisting that if you don't behave in certain ways or conform to her expectations, she will terminate your treatment. Like most Extreme Narcissists, she has a high need for control.

Once you get to know these narcissistic therapists on a personal rather than a professional level, you usually find their private lives to be a disaster. Broken marriages, alienated children, alcoholism, et cetera. They rely on adoration from their clients and junior colleagues to ward off private shame.

Ministers, preachers, rabbis, and other religious figures may also exploit their congregations in a similar way. In theory, it is having special access to spiritual truth that qualifies one for the ministry, drawing those who have a genuine calling, but it also appeals to Know-It-All Narcissists who want to be seen as superior and enlightened. The chance to stand on an elevated platform and deliver Truth to parishioners beneath him appeals deeply to the Know-It-All Narcissist. He thrives on the feeling of power and control he exercises as a result of what he (supposedly) knows. When charismatic, the narcissist in the pulpit often promotes a cultlike atmosphere within his congregation.

Over the last several decades, a number of charismatic televangelists have built enormous cult followings only to be exposed as liars and Extreme Narcissists who ruthlessly exploited their congregations for personal gain. Robert Tilton and Jim Bakker both fell from grace once their apparent godliness was revealed to be a fraud. While purporting to offer enlightenment, these men actually bilked their followers of millions of dollars in order to support their own lavish (and immoral) lifestyles.

In the guise of guru or wise man, the Know-It-All Narcissist taps into our need for heroes and our longing for saviors. He also exploits our built-in deference to leaders, the way "we are programmed to obey authority" by our genetic inheritance.[1] "With a leader, especially one who claims to have a sublime mission, as with a doctor or a priest or a parent, we tend to bestow the qualities of the role on the individual, and to follow the individual accordingly."[2] This predisposition to believe and obey our leaders makes us vulnerable to manipulation by the Know-It-All Narcissist offering psychological guidance or spiritual enlightenment.

The New Age movement has also produced its share of Know-It-All Narcissists. Bhagwan Shree Rajneesh and Sathya Sai Baba are but two of the many gurus revered by their cults as men of special enlightenment who were later charged with financial improprieties and sexual exploitation by many of their followers. More recently, Bikram Choudhury, founder of the eponymous Bikram Yoga movement, has become a cult guru surrounded by such followers as George Clooney, Madonna, Lady Gaga, Brooke Shields, and many other celebrities. His students view him not only as "a fully realized human being, a true master," but also as a visionary who can see into the future as well as the past. When he walks into a room, people will "put their hands together in prayer and get down on the floor and bow down, out of respect for him." Choudhury encourages such devotion, "regularly likening himself to Jesus Christ and Buddha. He often describes his yoga as the one true yoga, and all other yoga modalities as 'shit.'"[3]

Choudhury lives in an 8,000-square-foot mansion in Beverly Hills and owns dozens of Rolls-Royces and Bentleys, as well as a Daimler with a toilet in the back that once belonged to Howard Hughes.

When he teaches, he stands above his students wearing signature black Speedos, a jewel-encrusted Rolex, and a headset microphone, delivering a stream-of-consciousness monologue laced with sexual innuendo and hazing. He "is given to swaggering pronouncements—e.g., 'I have balls like atom bombs, two of them, 100 mega-tons each. Nobody fucks with me.'" He also makes grandiose claims for his yoga, "asserting that it cures cancer, rid Janet Reno of her Parkinson's, and saved John McEnroe's career, among other miracle tales." [4]

To make such claims persuasively, the man must have enormous charisma that doesn't translate onto the printed page.

In recent years, Choudhury has been sued by at least five former members of his inner circle on grounds of sexual abuse and rape. Choudhury denies the allegations. Exploiting their devotion to him as enlightened teacher, he at first made these women feel special by singling them out from his other students. Drawing on techniques from the Seductive Narcissist playbook, he took one student aside after class and said, "There were hundreds of bodies in that room tonight but you were the only one that listened to me. . . . Put your mat up front and close to me every class." He later told her, "You will be greater than Mother Teresa, but you have to follow me. You have to do everything I tell you to do." This "everything" involved brushing his hair and giving him increasingly sexual massages. He later managed to get her alone and allegedly raped her. [5]

Despite his obvious narcissism—that grandiose sense of self and lack of empathy—Choudhury's yoga methods have apparently helped many people turn their lives around during dark times. Even followers who know about the scandals and have personally witnessed the inappropriate behavior try to separate the method from the man, preserving what is truly valuable. Here is the odd paradox of the Know-It-All Narcissist: Driven to build and sustain his grandiose sense of self, he often achieves something of lasting value.

Sometimes these individuals are highly educated, well-informed people who really do know more than almost everyone else. When driven and naturally gifted, they may achieve great things. But in the process, they tend to treat their employees with contempt and refuse to share credit. By insisting that they always know best, they broadcast their winner self-image and make everyone else into comparative losers. Utterly lacking in humility, they announce again and again that they are the smartest, most insightful, most creative person in the room.

And sometimes they actually are.

THINK DIFFERENT

People who worked closely with Steve Jobs had a special name for his uncanny ability to impose his vision upon others. With reference to an early *Star Trek* episode, his colleagues at Apple called it the *reality distortion field*. Andy Hertzfeld, a member of the Macintosh team, describes it as "a confounding mélange of a charismatic rhetorical style, indomitable will, and an eagerness to bend any fact to fit the purpose at hand."[6] According to biographer Walter Isaacson, Jobs "would assert something—be it a fact about world history or a recounting of who suggested an idea at a meeting—without even considering the truth. It came from willfully defying reality, not only to others but to himself."[7]

Jobs found it difficult to acknowledge that other people in his employ might also have creative ideas; he often usurped their suggestions and took credit for having thought of them. Bud Tribble, another member of the Macintosh team, has said of Jobs that "[i]f you tell him a new idea, he'll usually tell you that he thinks it's stupid. But then, if he actually likes it, exactly one week later, he'll come back to you and propose your idea to you, as if he thought of it."[8] A Know-It-All Narcissist of the very first order, Jobs believed that he almost always knew more than anyone else in the room. He saw himself as a superior intellect on a par with Einstein, but also as a spiritually enlightened being such as Gandhi or the gurus he had met in India.[9]

He had a "binary way of categorizing things. People were either 'enlightened' or 'an asshole.'"[10] If you fell into the latter category, he would treat you with utter contempt. He would mock you, call you stupid, or deliberately humiliate you in front of your colleagues. Jobs had an "almost willful lack of tact" and couldn't "resist showing off his brutal, withering intelligence whenever he [was] around someone" he viewed as inferior.[11] Here we have the winner-loser dynamic inherent in narcissism, imposed upon the world of technological innovators. Jobs saw himself as the number one winner and regularly made the people around him feel like losers.

Former Apple employee Joanna Hoffman captures the dynamic well. "He had the uncanny capacity to know exactly what your weak point is, know what will make you feel small, to make you cringe," she says. "It's a common trait in people who are charismatic and know how to manipulate people. Knowing that he can crush you makes you feel weakened and eager for his approval, so then he can elevate you and put you on a pedestal and own you."[12] Many colleagues who knew Jobs well have identified a need to control other people and the events around him as the most prominent feature of his personality. Sometimes he would seduce people to do his bidding by idealizing them; or, more often, he would bully them into submission.

Like other Extreme Narcissists, Jobs believed the usual rules didn't apply to him. From early in grade school, it became clear that he "was not disposed to accept authority."[13] He flouted rules and defied his teachers; his parents never punished or disciplined him for his transgressions. As an adult, he would drive his car without license plates and make use of parking spaces reserved for the handicapped. He once got a ticket for driving over 100 miles per hour, was warned by the police officer that he would be put in jail if caught speeding again, then accelerated back to 100 as soon as the officer had left. Jobs also felt contempt for the ordinary rules governing social relationships: He failed to show up for meetings he had scheduled, arrived uninvited at friends' homes expecting them to give him dinner, and telephoned colleagues in the middle of the night to discuss a pressing idea.

Jobs was famous for his "empathy deficiency," as Isaacson describes it.[14] For five years, he dated and then lived with a woman named Tina Redse, who told Isaacson "how incredibly painful it was to be in love with someone so self-centered. Caring deeply about someone who seemed incapable of caring was a particular kind of hell she wouldn't wish on anyone."[15] Years later, she came across a description of Narcissistic Personality Disorder in a psychiatric manual and felt it described Steve Jobs to a T. "I think the issue is empathy—the capacity for empathy is lacking."[16]

Del Yocam, a longtime colleague, believes that Jobs's lack of empathy and "his desire for complete control for whatever he makes

derive directly from . . . the fact that he was abandoned at birth."
Joanne Schieble, Jobs's biological mother, was a graduate student
whose parents opposed her desire to marry Abdulfattah Jandali, a
Muslim teaching assistant from Syria, despite the fact that she was
pregnant. Under extreme pressure, she put her baby up for adoption
(though she eventually married Jandali). Jobs's first serious girlfriend,
Chrisann Brennan, says that being put up for adoption left Jobs "full
of broken glass."[17] Andy Herzfeld concurs: "The key question about
Steve is why he can't control himself at times from being so reflexively cruel and harmful to some people. . . . That goes back to being
abandoned at birth. The real underlying problem was the theme of
abandonment in Steve's life."

In his early thirties, after his adoptive mother had died, Jobs
eventually tracked down Schieble and built a relationship with her.
At that time, he learned that he also had a full sister (the writer Mona
Simpson) and that Jandali had abandoned mother and child when
Mona was five years old. After Simpson finally succeeded in locat-
ing Jandali, Jobs refused to meet him and rebuffed all overtures for
contact. "I was a wealthy man by then," Jobs explained, "and I didn't
trust him not to try to blackmail me or go to the press about it."[18]
Like Lance Armstrong, Jobs contemptuously dismissed his father as
a sperm donor. His biological parents "were my sperm and egg bank.
That's not harsh, it's just the way it was, a sperm bank thing, nothing
more."[19]

By insisting that separation from his birth mother made absolutely no difference in his development, Jobs echoes the commonly
held belief that adoption at birth is not traumatic to the infant. In
truth, as social workers and researchers have determined over the last
sixty years, adoption is *always* traumatic for the infant to some degree.

Even if it occurs at birth, it disrupts the attachment relationship that has been developing during pregnancy:

> Many doctors and psychologists now understand that bonding [between mother and infant] doesn't begin at birth, but is a continuum of physiological, psychological, and spiritual events which begin in utero and continue throughout the postnatal bonding period. When this natural evolution is interrupted by a postnatal separation from the biological mother, the resultant experience of abandonment and loss is indelibly imprinted upon the unconscious minds of these children, causing that which I call the "primal wound."[20]

This "primal wound" inflicted upon the budding psyche lies at the heart of core shame. Early trauma leaves the growing child with a sense that something has gone terribly wrong with his or her development, often leading to the kind of defensive character structure epitomized by Steve Jobs. It comes as no surprise that psychoanalyst Otto Kernberg identifies adopted children as one of five groups at especially high risk of developing Narcissistic Personality Disorder.[21]

Despite his well-known obnoxious personality and problematic relationship with the truth, Steve Jobs has remained a hero to millions following his death. Bikram Choudhury continues to attract a following of devoted students who revere him while the lawsuits work their way through the courts. One was a creative genius who largely shaped our relationship with modern technology, the other is a guru whose methods seem to have helped thousands of people turn their lives around. Apparently, we are willing to forgive the Know-It-All

Narcissist for his grandiose nature and lack of empathy provided that he offers us something of exceptional value.

How to Cope with the Know-It-All Narcissist

Self-absorbed bores like Monica are easy to spot and usually easy to avoid (unless they belong to your family); but when you're unable to escape them, you may find yourself becoming hostile or antagonistic. You might want to "shoot them down": At that tedious banquet I attended, I eventually found myself arguing with much of what Monica said, simply because I felt annoyed by her constant presumption that she knew better than the rest of us. Driven by the winner-loser dynamic, the Know-It-All Narcissist forces us to assume an inferior role, and we naturally want to turn the tables. I made a couple of ironic jokes at Monica's expense that night (they were met with laughter and relief by the other parents), but I felt bad about them later.

Rather than engaging in a *who's-up-who's-down* kind of struggle, bear in mind that what motivates the Know-It-All Narcissist is shame—even if you can't see it. Armed with this understanding, you might even come to feel some sympathy for a person who so relentlessly needs to build and defend a superior sense of self. Like the lady who "doth protest too much," her continuous assertion that she knows more than you betrays an underlying doubt about her worth as a person.

The Know-It-All Narcissist in the workplace presents a greater challenge because you have no choice but to engage with him. Often the best course of action is to ignore his "helpful" suggestions or to offer polite thanks and move on. A direct challenge will most likely lead to an escalating battle for supremacy. You may also try to disarm the Know-It-All Narcissist by inviting him to "step down" from his superior perch: Model humility and express a flexible point of view. Be open to his views without necessarily endorsing them. It also helps to have a sense of humor: If you're not triggered by his superior or condescending manner, you might find the Know-It-All Narcissist a bit absurd and ultimately harmless.

As priest, therapist, or guru, the Know-It-all Narcissist presents a more dangerous threat and a greater challenge because we're predisposed to believe in him. Coping with this type of narcissist involves staying awake, so to speak, and continuing to think for yourself. Of course it's beguiling to believe that someone else has the answers. Finding one's way in life is a challenge for all of us. Bearing emotional confusion and spiritual doubt can be a painful experience; you may therefore feel eager to entrust yourself to a therapist or guru who will light the way forward. Without quite acknowledging it to yourself, you may long to relinquish authority for your own life to someone who appears to have the answers.

Remain skeptical. When you notice behaviors that seem inconsistent with the role of spiritual or psychological guide, don't rationalize them away. Don't let your predisposition to defer to authority cloud your judgment. Coping with this type of Extreme Narcissist once again means turning inward and knowing yourself well. Many of us long to be saved, to believe someone else has profound insight and can tell us the answers; but in the end, we still have to think for ourselves.

8

"I'M RIGHT AND YOU'RE WRONG"
The Self-Righteous Narcissist

After school one afternoon, Fiona Googled the phrase *cruelty to animals* and, as she liked to tell it, "my life changed forever. I understood what I was meant to do." Only eleven years old at the time, she spent hours learning about the ASPCA, PETA, and other organizations devoted to animal rights. With horror, she read about the nightmare of industrial slaughterhouses, the abuse of laboratory animals in the pharmaceutical industry, and the dreadful lives led by circus animals. Ingrid Newkirk, co-founder of PETA, became a hero to Fiona. One night at the family dinner table, not long after her twelfth birthday, she announced her decision to become a vegetarian.

"Eat what you want," said her mother, "but don't expect me to make you any special meals."

"Animals have feelings, too," Fiona explained, "just like people, and knowing what I know now, I can't go on eating them. It's not

159

right." She glared pointedly at the plates sitting before the other members of her family, laden with roast pork.

Her brother, Miles, six years older and a senior in high school, gave her a smile of feigned admiration. In unctuous tones, he told her, "You're such a *good* person, Fiona. When I grow up, I want to be just like you. No, really—I mean it."

Their father and mother both laughed. Fiona often felt on the outside of her family, not so sharp-witted or verbal. Her dry, no-nonsense mother had made clear she was an "accident" and that they hadn't planned on having a second child. For as long as she could remember, Fiona had felt unwanted.

Alone in her room after dinner, she imagined subjecting Miles to the sort of torture regularly inflicted upon lab animals. It would serve him right for being such a jerk.

During high school, Fiona became a campus radical, pursuing one cause after another. With several like-minded followers, she once mounted a protest over the lack of vegetarian and vegan options in the cafeteria. When the administration paid them no heed, her group finally invaded the principal's office, staging a sit-in that made the local evening news. "Vegetarians have rights, too!" she told the TV cameras. Fiona posted a link to the news clip on her Facebook page with the caption: "They're Finally Paying Attention!!!"

While she collaborated with other students on a number of pro-tests, Fiona had no close friends. From time to time, she'd develop an intense connection with another girl, usually a passionate devotee to one of her causes, but they'd eventually fall out when the new friend questioned Fiona's judgment or argued for a less confrontational approach.

"You're either with me or against me," Fiona often said.

One such friendship abruptly ended when the other girl's family bought a pedigreed puppy from a local breeder. When shown a picture of the adorable dog, Fiona flew into a rage.

"Having a pet is no different from slavery, in my opinion. But you could've at least adopted a dog from the shelter. It is so *wrong* to support puppy mills when thousands of sheltered animals need a home!"

After the girl began to argue, she was abruptly banished from Fiona's animal rights club.

At the beginning of her last year in high school, Fiona turned vegan. Miles, home from law school for Thanksgiving, made his usual sarcastic remarks about her eating habits, but Fiona didn't rise to the bait. While her mother prepared the traditional meal, she made herself a maximum nuisance preparing her own repast of brown rice, squash, kale, and black beans. Following grace, Fiona told her family members she felt especially grateful this year that she could enjoy the holiday without sacrificing innocent creatures. She gave them all a beatific smile.

His mouth loaded with turkey, Miles said, "Did you know that growing wheat or rice kills twenty-five times more animals per gram of usable protein than farming red meat?" He'd obviously read up on the subject and was prepared for just such a moment. "When you clear the land for agriculture, you wipe out all the frogs and mice and snakes that live there. They're animals, too, you know."

Fiona glowered at him but said nothing. When she went away to college the following year, she limited communication with her parents and completely broke off contact with Miles.

At the age of nineteen she had her first romantic relationship, with Cooper, another vegan with whom she co-founded a local chapter of PETA. Together, they staged a number of public demonstrations that garnered media attention. But when Fiona decided to replicate Ingrid Newkirk's infamous protest—hanging herself naked from a meat hook inside the student union, as if she were a cow carcass— Cooper told her she was going too far.

"Either support my beliefs or take a walk," Fiona replied.

"You care more about getting attention than about your causes," Cooper fumed.

"Fuck you!" she cried.

They broke up, and Cooper renounced his position with their PETA chapter. When other members asked about his departure, Fiona called him weak and insincere. "For him, it was just a fad."

"DO YOU EVER THINK ABOUT WHAT *I* NEED?"

Many vegans and vegetarians passionately believe that consuming meat is immoral, but Fiona's attitude toward her friends and family members reflects a holier-than-thou kind of self-righteousness. Not only does she disagree with them but she believes her views are superior to and more virtuous than theirs. She is right and they are wrong. She is a "good" person; if people challenge her, they are "bad" and she cuts them dead. But as ex-boyfriend Cooper suggested, her desire for media attention sometimes seems a more potent motivator than moral conviction. She needs other people to *see* her and acknowledge her superiority.

The Self-Righteous Narcissist shows up in many walks of life, particularly within organized religion. Many people hold deeply cherished beliefs, but the narcissistic believer insists on flaunting her devotion, as if that makes her a superior person. She wants to be admired for the intensity of her faith. She often passes judgment on

162

other people while giving lip service to Christian charity. She makes an ostentatious show of supporting worthy causes, heading committees, or spearheading initiatives that garner attention. Within her immediate family, she is both emotionally neglectful and demanding. She frequently feuds with relatives and holds grudges against them, coming across as harsh or lacking in empathy.

My client Winona was married to a man who believed himself to be spiritually enlightened and superior. Mark spent many hours devoted to the study of Scripture and frequently told Winona what Bible study had revealed to him about her defects as a wife. If they had a fight, he invariably told her that she was wrong and that if she would only turn more toward God's Word as he had done, she would see the error of her ways. If she ever presumed to criticize his behavior, he would launch an immediate counterassault on her character.

Mark had put in place a thrice-weekly schedule for having sex, regardless of whether Winona wanted it. He also told her that according to the Bible, household chores and child rearing were "woman's work." Whenever it suited him, he went off to attend religious retreats without considering his wife and children. On the few occasions when Winona complained about his neglect of her needs, he immediately turned the tables. "You're always talking about *your* needs. What about mine? Do you ever think about me and what *I* need?"

Winona and Mark finally went for pastoral counseling with leaders of their church. In the beginning, the church leaders tried to remain neutral; but over time, as the depth of Mark's selfishness and insensitivity became clear, they eventually supported Winona in her desire for a divorce. For months thereafter, Mark sent repeated emails to the pastor and counselors with whom they had worked, accusing them of spiritual dereliction in their pastoral duties. He made himself out to be a martyr betrayed by church elders. He insisted that, in God's eyes, he was an innocent man who had been wronged.

Over the years, many of my clients have spent sessions describing their marital fights, angrily recounting the ways they had been mistreated or misjudged by their spouses. I've listened to righteously indignant diatribes that reminded me of legal presentations before the court, where my client made an open-and-shut case against the offending spouse, "proving" him or her to be entirely in the wrong. It has often felt to me as if my clients were painting themselves as *extremely good* people—virtuous victims superior to their *very bad* spouses.

This type of argument often takes place in relationships that began with extreme mutual idealization. As I discussed in Chapter Five, romantic love is a semidelusional state of mind where two people agree that they are the most attractive, fascinating people in the world. They become the center of one another's universe and often idealize each other to a significant degree. In due course, the idealization fades and the partners develop a more realistic view of the other person, along with a more down-to-earth kind of love. But men and women who rely on narcissistic defenses against shame cannot bear to be more fully and accurately "seen." As mutual idealization begins to fail, it falls apart along polarized lines, whereby each partner lays claim to winner status and makes the other one into the loser. In the brutal language of harsh morality, they often rage against each other with righteous indignation.

Following a heated argument with her husband, Eric, my client Denise would spend sleepless hours reviewing the exchange in a highly accusatory way, going over all of Eric's faults and progressing to total character assassination in her mind. She'd spend the opening minutes of her next session recounting the fight in black-and-white terms. Although she didn't always spell it out, she believed that by virtue of her many years in therapy, she possessed greater insight and self-awareness than Eric, who supposedly knew nothing about himself or the destructive ways in which he behaved. She was superior and enlightened while he remained in the dark. She was right and he was wrong.

Denise had come from an extremely troubled family; when I began seeing her as a young woman, she already had a long history of drug abuse and self-destructive behavior. Over the years, she'd made great progress as a result of our work: She finished college, developed a career, married another professional, and gave birth to children. Like many people in flight from shame, however, she had developed a kind of defensive post-therapy identity: Whereas before, she had often felt inferior to other people because of her troubled family background and early struggles, she now saw herself as superior (a psychoanalytic winner) due to all the insight she had gained through our work together. Unenlightened Eric often found himself cast in the role of loser.

Underneath (unconsciously), Denise felt ashamed and guilty about the "crazy" way she instigated these fights. In her relentless goal to become Winner Denise, she refused to recognize her limits and often took on more than she could manage in her daily life. As a result, she tended to deteriorate under pressure, becoming more forgetful, irritable, prone to angry outbursts, intolerant of the emotional needs of her family, et cetera. Insomnia plagued her. Instead of feeling regret about poor choices she had made, she found fault with Eric, endlessly nitpicking until she provoked a fight.

Denise saw the issue in terms of black and white: Either (1) she was entirely right and Eric to blame for everything; or (2) she was such a messed-up nutcase that we might as well give up and flush her down the toilet. Because acknowledging her own contribution to these fights reconnected her to shame, she usually defended her self-image as Winner Denise with great zeal. Under assault, Eric often responded in kind, calling her "crazy" and treating her with contempt. Early on, if I tried to promote a more nuanced view, she would turn on me as well, accusing me of insensitivity or "teaming up" with Eric against her. On the verge of divorce, Eric entered therapy with one of my closest colleagues.

Denise and Eric's marriage survived because both learned to defuse the winner-loser dynamic that characterized their fights. Over time, Denise became better able to endure her shame, acknowledge her limitations, and take better care of herself. Marriage to a fully Self-Righteous Narcissist rarely ends so well. Throughout prolonged divorce proceedings and child custody disputes marked by their savagery, Tina Swithin's ex-husband, Seth, maintained a stance of wronged virtue: He insisted he was an upstanding man who always behaved in an upright manner, while she was an unprincipled and manipulative "slut" without morals or proper values.

For most people, the end of a marriage or long-term relationship feels like a painful narcissistic injury. The withdrawal of a partner's love and admiration usually *hurts*, especially when unexpected, and we often feel humiliated or shamed by the experience (think back to Kitty's reaction when she realizes that Vronsky has lost interest in her). When the object of our affection decides we no longer deserve their love, our self-esteem is shaken. We may doubt our value as a person and retreat from the world, licking our wounds in private. Over time, we grieve the end of the relationship and, in the process, slowly recover our sense of self-worth.

On the other hand, if we cannot bear the shame that comes with rejection, we may respond with narcissistic defenses, turning the other person into an unworthy loser. When Natalie (see Chapter Two) hears the phone message from her boyfriend and realizes he intends to dump her, the hurt lasts only a second before mutating into righteous anger: "Men are such assholes!" Nobody takes well to rejection; we understand and sympathize with her reaction because we know she's in pain. Maybe she'll grieve the relationship later, when she's not so beset.

The Self-Righteous Narcissist never grieves. Instead, he blames. For years after their marriage had ended, Winona's husband, Mark, maintained his martyr status. You probably have firsthand experience with this phenomenon in your own life. Like me, you might have listened to an acquaintance vilify a former spouse, depicting the ex as a person with absolutely no redeeming qualities, and wondered whether there was another side to the story. As the abuse piled up, you might have wanted to say "But you once loved this person." The spouse who has been betrayed is particularly prone to this kind of righteous indignation, where feelings of humiliation lead to the kind of narcissistic defenses against shame we have come to recognize.

Donald Nathanson describes this dynamic in terms of *disgust* (one of the innate affects). "In the interpersonal world," he explains, "wherever there is disgust there will be gross alteration of self-esteem or in our esteem for another person. Divorce can be experienced as victory if we view ourselves as perfect and the other as the pure object of disgust."[1] In other words, we ward off the shame of rejection (the "gross alteration of self-esteem") by developing feelings of disgust for the person we once loved. According to Nathanson, such disgust often expresses itself in *contempt*, "a form of anger in which we declare the other person . . . as far beneath us and worthy only of rejection."[2] Thus contempt, one of the primary narcissistic defenses against shame, turns the other person into a loser, while we pass judgment from on high.

This explanation may help to clear up some puzzling contradictions in the behavior of Mel Gibson. His abusive, racist, misogynistic, and above all self-righteous rants against former girlfriend Oksana Grigorieva make him seem like a narcissistic Neanderthal of the first order. His anti-Semitic remarks to a Malibu police officer in July 2006 sound like the opinions of a world-class bigot who feels superior and full of contempt. And yet close friends are quick to defend him. Within the Hollywood film community, "hardly anyone has a bad word to say about him. Most describe a boon companion and recount acts of surprising generosity on Gibson's part."[3] Many Jews, gays, and blacks count him among their friends and insist he is not homophobic, anti-Semitic, or racist.

While Gibson has made other troubling remarks over the course of his career, these two most egregious examples came during relationship breakups. Before launching into his tirade against that Malibu police officer, Gibson announced that his wife intended to divorce him. "My life is over," he said. "I'm fucked. Robyn's going to leave me."[4] One close friend believes that, when the officer pulled him over, Gibson "felt that he had just absolutely failed as a human being."[5] We can see his abusive behavior toward the officer as an attempt to offload the unbearable shame he felt at being a loser.

Although Gibson's defense of those recorded phone conversations with Grigorieva makes light of their brutality, he's right to suggest that we should "put it all in the proper context of being in an irrationally heated discussion at the height of a breakdown."[6] If you listen to the recordings of those calls, widely available on the Internet, you can hear the agony in his voice.[7] The words he speaks are highly offensive, but the tone betrays a man who is suffering deeply. Gibson was drowning in shame: His long marriage had failed, and his next relationship turned out to be a disaster. No doubt he felt like a total loser and defended himself against it with blame, contempt, and righteous indignation.

Of course, his well-known struggles with alcoholism also played a part in the demise of both relationships. We'll discuss the role of shame in fueling addictive behavior in Chapter Ten.

THE NARCISSISTIC BIGOT

The person with racist attitudes may have absorbed those views from the world around him: Racist societies often institutionalize and covertly school their citizens in intolerance. But in other cases, individuals like Mel Gibson hold racist views that directly conflict with the values of their social milieu. In order to make sense of such people, we must look to the dynamics of narcissism: The racist is sometimes a narcissist who boosts his self-image at the expense of racial and minority groups he places beneath him.

I am a winner and you, as a member of Group X, are a loser.

Bullying Narcissists (see Chapter Three) often hold racist attitudes and persecute minorities with righteous zeal. "Feeling superior to their targets, they believe that they have both the ability and the right to abuse them. They are also proselytizers convinced that only they have the truth and that their way is the one and only right one . . .

169

that they are pure and others foul."[8] In short, the Self-Righteous Narcissist with racist attitudes views himself as enlightened and his victims as inferior, contemptible losers who deserve whatever they get. Like all Extreme Narcissists, he is decidedly lacking in empathy.

The self-righteousness of the bigot embodies a narcissistic defense against some feared or hated aspect of the self that has been disavowed and projected onto the "inferior" other. Homophobia provides a useful and familiar example. For many years, professional and armchair psychologists have speculated that people who express strongly homophobic attitudes secretly harbor same-sex attractions, and several studies have recently provided empirical evidence that this is actually true.[9] In order to preserve their idealized heterosexual self-image, homophobes disavow their own attractions and then despise those feelings "inside" of other people, so to speak.

The homophobe often expresses his intolerance of homosexual behavior and sexual relations with self-righteous superiority, conveyed in the language of religious belief. The case of George Rekers provides an illuminating example. A psychologist and ordained Southern Baptist minister, Rekers has devoted much of his career to the conversion of young gay men to a heterosexual lifestyle. He advocates a type of psychotherapy that uses aversive counterconditioning to punish behaviors that don't conform to gender stereotypes and to reward those that do. Rekers is so certain of the correctness of his views that he has testified in numerous high-profile cases about the immorality and destructiveness of homosexuality, calling it sinful and contrary to God's law.

In 2010, Rekers was photographed with a male escort named Lucien whom he had hired from Rentboy.com, supposedly to carry his luggage on a European tour. Although Rekers claimed he had no idea the boy was a prostitute, Lucien later gave interviews insisting that he had been hired to provide sexual massages while in the nude. Another escort and former porn star, Carl Shepherd, claimed he had been hired for similar services in 1992 and provided insight into Rekers's tormented psychology. After the massage had ended and Rekers asked him about his porn career, Shepherd gave intimate details. Rekers "seemed really disgusted. His face curled up. He handed me $150 and I left. But I felt a bit guilty it had ended like that. I remember thinking that I'd really grossed him out."[10]

According to classic psychoanalytic theory, disgust often embodies a *reaction formation*—a type of psychological defense against forbidden or unacceptable impulses. In order to disown his shame-ridden homosexual self, Rekers developed feelings of disgust for his own sexual desires, constructed an idealized false (heterosexual) self, and devoted his entire professional life to the argument that people with those very same inclinations were defective and sinful. He became a righteous crusader against homosexuality, passing himself off as a respected authority while lying to himself and everyone else about his true nature.

When he spends his career on the big stage—in politics, the entertainment industry, or professional athletics—the Self-Righteous Narcissist has a powerful platform for the expression of his contempt and the disavowal of his own shame. Sometimes, as in the case of George Rekers, Ted Haggard, or Larry Craig, their righteousness takes a religious tone that masks their contempt. Feigned humility and an apparent devotion to Scripture and "traditional" moral values may conceal the true purpose of their crusades: to support a defensive and idealized self-image that keeps shame at bay.

But sometimes, the self-righteous disdain for other people is all too blatant. Rather than hiding behind a mask of virtue, some prominent narcissists cast humility aside, using their power and position to express contempt while inflating their own grandiose self-image. And although self-righteousness usually connotes a sense of moral or religious superiority, an Extreme Narcissist without religious convictions can nonetheless come across as self-righteous. Some narcissists express themselves in self-righteous ways because they believe that they understand better than everyone else what needs to be done or which opinions to hold. Rather than relying on Scripture or traditional moral values, they view *themselves* as the ultimate source of authority.

Like the Bullying Narcissist who persecutes his victims in order to support his own winner status, the Self-Righteous Narcissist with a public bullhorn needs an opponent he can humiliate to demonstrate his superior understanding. In positions of power, he may publicly abuse his employees and treat them with scorn. He often picks fights and mounts highly publicized feuds, "proving" his own superiority by ridiculing his enemies as losers, idiots, and whiners. And like the Know-It-All Narcissist, he must always be in the right.

WINNER TAKE ALL

Fred Trump, Donald's father, expected his sons to be ruthless competitors who showed their opponents no mercy. "Be a killer," he told them. Like Tiger Woods's father, Fred Trump believed there were only two classes of people in the world—winners and losers; every Trump would of course be a winner. As a real estate developer in the Bronx, Fred had already made millions of dollars, following in the footsteps of his own highly successful father. He expected nothing less from his sons, Fred Jr. (Freddy), Donald, and Robert.

Though the oldest son was groomed to step into his father's shoes, Freddy didn't seem to fit the mold. An old school chum describes him as "a real pussycat, not mean and aggressive, kind of pathetic, really."[11] Once Freddy entered the family business, his father would publicly chew him out when he made mistakes and withhold praise when he did well. If Freddy showed vulnerability or fear in his presence, it would send his father into a contemptuous rage. Fred also viewed his son as a "wimp" because of his intellectual interests. Freddy began to smoke and drink heavily, eventually dying at the age of forty-two "from a massive heart attack caused by alcoholism so acute that it verged on the suicidal."[12]

Donald might have suffered a similar fate had he not turned out to be the killer that Fred expected. From an early age, Donald was hypercompetitive and always needed to be the best at whatever he did. He also displayed a defiant attitude toward authority so troubling his parents finally sent him away to New York Military Academy (NYMA), an institution renowned for its ability to "curb unruly young spirits."[13] There, Donald shaped up and threw himself into sport with a competitive fervor, though he had no close friends. "I think it was because he was too competitive, and with a friend you don't always compete," says Ted Levin, Donald's roommate at NYMA. "It was like he had this defensive wall around him, and he wouldn't let anyone get close."[14]

Unlike Fred, who made a fortune constructing middle-income housing in the Bronx, Donald had his eyes on Manhattan. Unlike Fred, who eschewed publicity and quietly forged political alliances behind the scenes, Donald wanted to be famous. And unlike Fred, who was "shy and uncomfortable in person,"[15] Donald was brash and expansive. "He seemed like an epic character, straight out of Stendhal," recalls Ned Eichler, a former business school professor who negotiated with Donald on one of his earliest deals. "An ambitious boy from the provinces, full of his own ego, wanting to make his way in the city."[16]

From the outset of his career, Trump was flagrantly grandiose, with a tendency to exaggerate so marked that he often discarded truth in order to create the impression he preferred. He would invariably describe his latest projects in superlative terms—the *tallest* building in the world, the *biggest* development in New York, the *largest* real estate acquisition ever recorded in the city, the most glamorous, luxurious, expensive apartments available, and on and on. "No matter the occasion, he was always competing, always concentrating on how to make whatever he was doing seem bigger and better than what anyone else had ever done. When he lost, he would say he won; when he won, he would say he won more."[17]

The actual truth didn't matter, and if anyone challenged his version of events, he would go on the attack. Donald Trump always had to be right. In the early 1990s, as the real estate market collapsed and his empire seemed about to implode under the weight of excessive debt, he blamed many of his closest advisors and employees, including those who had strongly advised against his riskier ventures. "He could not acknowledge his refusal to heed their warnings or accept responsibility for the problems that had resulted from his own actions."[18] One by one, he fired them or pushed them out. He refused to pay their bills.

Exploiting media access, he heaped scorn upon his enemies—that is, those people who disagreed with him or didn't do what he wanted. Early in his career, when Mayor Ed Koch declined to give him enormous tax concessions to build a megaproject called Television City, Trump "blasted the mayor as a 'moron,' called for his impeachment, and demanded an investigation of Koch's involvement in his appointees' misdeeds."[19] At a public hearing for approval of another development, when a local resident argued that Trump was playing the taxpayers of New York "for small-town suckers," he erupted in rage. "That's all bullshit!" he said loudly. "That woman is a fat pig who doesn't know what she's talking about. It's a pack of lies!"[20]

Those who have worked closely with Trump are familiar with his blaming, self-righteous, and contemptuous management style. When things weren't going as Donald thought they should, he would erupt like a volcano, screaming, yelling profanities, hurling accusations of laziness and incompetence.[21] During the construction of an exclusive lounge for preferred customers at Trump Plaza, manager Steve Hyde had repeatedly explained to his boss that the ceiling would have to be lowered in some areas in order to accommodate plumbing for those luxury suites directly above. Because he knew Trump loathed low ceilings, he made sure his boss understood. On the day when Trump and other executives toured the new club with Hyde, he reacted with shock and indignation, as if Hyde had never said a word.

"What the fuck is this?" Trump said. "Who said to make this ceiling so low?"

"You knew about this, Donald," Hyde replied. "We talked about it, if you remember, and the plans—"

Abruptly Donald leaped up and punched his fist through the tile. Then he turned on Hyde in a rage. "You cocksucker! Motherfucker! Where the fuck were you? Where was your fucking head?" The tirade went on at great length as Trump "humiliated [Hyde] in front of twenty people, colleagues and professionals."[22]

Jack O'Donnell, Hyde's successor at Trump Plaza, experienced similar treatment. In the beginning of his tenure, he became accustomed to Trump's "brusque manner, which, like the characteristic smirk he always wore, was etched in his face."[23] For years, he swallowed hard and accepted the way Trump would ignore his advice and then blame him for the consequences. O'Donnell endured his contempt, his abusive rages, and his ingratitude. He listened as Trump dismissed one dissenter after another as an idiot, an asshole, a fucking moron, a little shit who had no idea what he was talking about.

O'Donnell finally reached his limit when Trump began to blame him for a series of crises that occurred around the opening of his biggest casino in Atlantic City, the Trump Taj Mahal. With rising indignation, Trump first accused him of negotiating a poor contract for a concert by the Rolling Stones against which O'Donnell had previously advised him. Trump went on to blame the bad Stones deal on O'Donnell's close friend and former co-worker Mark Etess, who had died not long before in a tragic helicopter accident. O'Donnell at last was fed up and rose to the defense of his friend.

Trump responded with a full-throated attack on O'Donnell's performance at the most profitable of his assets. "I'm fucking sick of the results down there, and I'm fucking sick of looking at bad numbers . . . and you telling me you can't do this, you can't do that . . . and I'm sick and fucking tired of you telling me no!"[24]

No longer able to endure Trump's self-righteous contempt and the continuous assaults on his character, O'Donnell resigned that very day.

How to Cope with the Self-Righteous Narcissist

As Jack O'Donnell learned from painful experience, the Self-Righteous Narcissist will not listen to reason and is immune to arguments based on truth and logic. He makes use of contempt and indignant rage in order to bolster his position and invalidate those who disagree with him. When mistakes or failure threaten his self-esteem, he will swiftly shift blame onto others. Rather than experience his own shame, he will force those people nearby to carry it for him by humiliating them.

When contending with a Self-Righteous Narcissist in the workplace, your unwritten job description often includes protecting him from shame. On a regular basis, you will need to assume responsibility for his mistakes. From time to time, you must endure humiliation so that he can preserve his idealized self-image. Don't bother trying to reason with him. He won't listen to fact-based assertions of the truth and he won't ever change. Although you may consider the way he treats you to be entirely unfair, bear in mind that within the narcissistic worldview, fairness is irrelevant.

One litigation attorney I know worked with a Self-Righteous Narcissist who regularly blamed her for his own mistakes. At first, she'd protest the injustice of his criticism, which usually intensified his blaming assault and brought on an angry tirade. She finally learned that the most effective strategy was to roll over and accept responsibility with a simple apology. "I'm really sorry. What can I do to fix the problem?" This approach took the indignant wind out of his sails, though it meant she had to swallow her pride. If you find yourself in a similar work situation, you'll have to decide whether advancing your career merits the degree of humiliation and suffering involved.

In friendships with a Self-Righteous Narcissist, you may be safe from attack as long as you remain a supportive ally of her idealized self-image. You will need to listen sympathetically when she tells you of her disagreements with other people, even if you believe those others aren't as entirely to blame as she makes them seem. Don't ever criticize her. While you may believe that authentic friendship involves truth-telling, the Self-Righteous Narcissist doesn't want to hear the truth. For that reason, you'll have to decide whether this "friendship" truly satisfies you. Is it worth enduring the reality distortions you must endorse? Do you really want to spend precious personal time holding your tongue?

In a romantic relationship, especially in the early idealizing period, you may not recognize that you're involved with a Self-Righteous Narcissist. You naturally enjoy being idealized and, at first, you may not question the harsh judgments he continually levels at other people. Because you're in love, you may want to be supportive, silencing any doubts you have about the fairness of his criticisms. Once you have your first major disagreement as a couple, you will then find yourself the object of the same harshness. This shift from idealization to savagery will likely come as a huge shock. You may feel a sense of grief at this romantic rupture.

Following a brutal argument of this kind, after time has passed and he feels more secure in his identity, the Self-Righteous Narcissist may become apologetic and try to reestablish a state of mutual idealization. In your unhappy state, grieving your lost romance, you may eagerly welcome his apology. You may forgive him, deceiving yourself that this argument was the result of a simple misunderstanding, a one-off spat that won't recur. After their early blowups, when Seth would savage Tina Swithin's self-esteem, he often sent her flowers and romantic notes the next day, begging forgiveness. It took her many months to recognize the pattern.

Like Tina Swithin, you must recognize that a relationship with a Self-Righteous Narcissist involves such repeated assaults and humiliation. Don't let your own longing for idealized love blind you.

"I'm Right and You're Wrong": The Self-Righteous Narcissist

Don't harbor any false hopes that your lover will change and you can recover romantic bliss. Like most Extreme Narcissists, this type rarely changes but instead relies on increasingly strident forms of blame, contempt, and indignant rage to bolster an idealized self-image, all at your expense.

9

"CHALLENGE ME AND I'LL HURT YOU"

The Vindictive Narcissist

In Edgar Allan Poe's macabre tale *The Cask of Amontillado*, Montresor, the story's first-person narrator, lures an unsuspecting friend named Fortunato down into his wine cellar. He first offers Fortunato enough wine to make him drunk, then chains him into an alcove, bricks over the opening, and leaves him there to die. The first sentence of the story provides his motivation: "The thousand injuries of Fortunato I had borne as I best could, but when he ventured upon insult, I vowed revenge."

Like Montresor, the Vindictive Narcissist is a person who experiences an injury to his "precious pride" as a personal attack and viciously retaliates. He has a notoriously thin skin, often taking offense where none is intended. His hostile response to innocent remarks often baffles those on the receiving end of his vindictiveness because it seems so out of proportion to the perceived insult. An aspect of human psychology introduced in Chapter Two helps to explain his behavior.

According to the *principle of false attribution*, human beings are inclined to infer agency where none exists: We often believe that if we are experiencing a particular emotion, someone else must be *deliberately* causing us to feel that way. As an example, I discussed the occasional irritability we all feel from time to time, and our tendency to experience other people as annoying in those moments, as if they are the *cause* of our feeling state. We may even feel persecuted by their behavior, as if they deliberately intend to get on our nerves.

When unconscious shame threatens to break through into awareness, the Vindictive Narcissist feels under attack. Core shame is a deeply painful experience, and due to the principle of false attribution, the Vindictive Narcissist believes that someone else *intends* her to feel that pain. For this reason, she may experience you as attacking her when you inadvertently do or say something that ignites her shame. Her response may seem irrational. "I didn't mean it that way!" you might want to argue. But like Montresor, who was immune to Fortunato's pleas for mercy as he bricked up the alcove, the Vindictive Narcissist won't listen. She might lash out to "hurt you back" or methodically devise ways to destroy you.

Given the winner-loser dynamic inherent in narcissism, it comes as no surprise that Extreme Narcissists make sore losers in both games and sports. Whenever losing in competition exposes them to shame, they may feel attacked and will resort to the narcissistic defenses we have come to recognize. They will refuse to take responsibility for their loss, blaming their teammates or accusing opponents of cheating. They will take refuge in superiority and contempt. They may become overwhelmed with indignant rage, attacking their adversaries in ways that may turn vindictive.

Like Tiger Woods, who berated his caddy after making a poor shot, the sore loser who feels threatened by shame may lash out at the nearest bystander, and they often do so in highly vicious ways. Within the world of professional tennis, John McEnroe was famous for abusing referees when a call didn't go his way.[1] Jimmy Connors regularly made headlines for his grandiose behavior and the verbal assaults he leveled at referees. Serena Williams, Andy Roddick, and Martina Hingis have all been labeled "sore losers" by aficionados of the sport. YouTube hosts many videos that record their reactions to adverse calls; in each case, the players attempt to humiliate the referee, treating him with utter contempt and taking refuge in self-righteous indignation. They often seem to feel persecuted and respond with a vindictive assault on the referee's character.

The Vindictive Narcissist also shows up in the workplace. Highly competitive, he imagines himself surrounded by rivals and becomes envious when someone else succeeds. He may feel wounded or take offense where none was offended. If he feels deeply threatened by a competitor, he may try to destroy that person's career or drive him from the company. His vindictiveness may persist long after his enemy has quit the field or been fired.

"YOU'LL NEVER WORK IN THIS TOWN AGAIN"

For six years after graduation from college, Tyler had worked in the marketing department of Dominion Enterprises, developing an expertise in online branding. He had received consistently positive performance reviews, working his way up the corporate ladder, and he now headed a small team of IT professionals who managed the company's website, email marketing, and search engine optimization efforts. During his tenure at Dominion, he'd always worked well with his colleagues and supervisors. When the head of marketing announced that he would be departing for a better opportunity, Tyler asked higher-ups to consider him for the position, though without much hope of getting the job. He knew he was underqualified.

Tyler was away at a trade show when he heard that Dominion had instead hired the head of marketing from a competitor, a man whom Tyler had never met. On his first day back from this trip, Tyler was entering his own personal office when he was stopped by Phil, the new head of marketing. He didn't immediately realize that this was his new boss.

"I need a report on the new Twitter campaign right away," Phil told him. "I have a meeting with the president this afternoon."

"I'm sorry," Tyler said, feeling a little jet-lagged. "And you are . . ."

As soon as the words were out of his mouth, Tyler realized who this must be. Phil looked deeply offended. He pulled back as his face gnarled in contempt.

"Your *boss*, genius," Phil snapped. "I want it by noon," he added, turning away.

Later in the morning when he dropped off his report, Tyler tried to apologize but Phil rebuffed him. From that point on, it seemed to Tyler that he could do nothing to please his new boss. When he submitted a plan for a series of how-to articles that would be hosted on the company website, Phil shot down the idea.

"We need to develop more video content instead."

"I agree. I've brought up the idea before. The problem is our budget—no money."

"Let me worry about the money. Just bring me a plan."

Tyler felt excited that he might finally get to produce videos for the website. He'd discussed the possibility many times with a friend who ran a small production company making inexpensive TV commercials for the local broadcast market. For days after his meeting with Phil, he worked hard to develop his proposal for a series of sixty-second shorts, putting together a budget with the help of his friend. When he hand-delivered it to his boss, Phil said, "What's this?"

"The plan for new video content on the website you asked for."

Phil handed it back. "There's no money in the budget."

"But you said you'd find a way."

"I said nothing of the kind."

Inside, Tyler was fuming, but he held his tongue. As he was walking out the door, Phil stopped him. "Hey McOwen, I hear you were after my job." Tyler turned back. Phil gave him a smug sort of grin.

"I guess the better man won," Tyler said, though it killed him to say it.

Phil's grin grew bigger. "Damn straight. Thank you, McOwen. You can go now."

Tyler felt so angry that he next made a major error in judgment. Without giving himself time to cool down, he sent an email to the president with a copy of his video proposal. "I know in prior discussions video seemed out of reach, but I've found a way to bring costs down. See my attached proposal and budget."

The following day, Phil stormed into Tyler's office, screaming so loudly that everyone on the floor must have heard.

"Don't you ever do a fucking end run around me again or I will rip your lungs out. I'll tear you open and leave you bleeding to death on

185

the floor. Is that clear enough for you, moron? Who the fuck do you think you are, going over my head? You little ass-wipe."

Tyler was speechless. He'd dealt with bad tempers and angry outbursts before—corporate life was rife with large egos—but this was a whole new level of abuse.

"You can't talk to me that way," he stammered.

"I'll talk to you any fucking way I like," Phil snarled. He stormed out of Tyler's office, slamming the door behind him.

Things went from bad to worse. Phil sent emails demanding constant progress reports and responded to them with profane mockery. Meetings of the marketing team were regularly held but Tyler rarely received notice. At the meetings he did attend, Phil treated him with blatant contempt, ridiculing his suggestions. One time, Phil even threw his pen at him. When Tyler looked around the conference table for support, his co-workers kept their gazes down. Phil had cowed them all and nobody wanted to incur his wrath.

Tyler was having trouble sleeping at nights now. In the mornings before he left for work, he sometimes felt so nauseated he was afraid he might throw up. When he finally left for a trade show in Los Angeles, he felt relieved to be away from the office; but even in California, he couldn't escape. Phil sent him hectoring emails, asking for daily reports that accounted for every second of his time. When he returned, Phil demanded an itemized expense report and challenged every item. He refused to reimburse Tyler for taxi fare from the airport, insisting he should have taken the hotel courtesy van instead.

Tyler felt so stressed that he finally decided to contact Bonnie, the head of human resources at Dominion. She didn't seem terribly sympathetic to his plight.

"If he's so bad, why haven't I received any other complaints?" she asked

"They're all afraid of him."

Bonnie eyed him skeptically. "Have you tried talking to him about the way he treats you?"

Tyler scoffed. "You don't talk to Phil. You listen. And yes, I've tried."

"I'll see what I can do," Bonnie told him, and he knew nothing would come of this meeting.

"I've got emails," he said, feeling desperate. "I have witnesses. I can prove what I'm saying is true."

From the look on her face, Tyler realized he had just become a problem employee who might file a lawsuit against the company. Now he was an enemy.

Tyler next consulted a lawyer, who advised him to start keeping a log of offensive encounters and to preserve their email exchanges. He also suggested that Tyler start looking for another job.

"But that means the asshole *wins*," Tyler objected.

"Don't go mano-a-mano with this guy—that's my advice. You'll lose."

One day when Phil once again ridiculed him in front of the entire marketing department, Tyler finally handed in his resignation. He gave two weeks' notice and contacted a headhunter who assured him he'd have no trouble finding a job, given his skill set and experience. After submitting Tyler for several positions without landing him an interview, she sounded less hopeful. "You're getting bad performance reviews from your last boss," the headhunter told him. "I gather he has it in for you."

That evening at home, Tyler received an email from Phil. "You'll never work in this town again." He signed it with an evil smiley-face grin.

In desperation, Tyler went back to his lawyer. They submitted a full incident report to human resources at Dominion with the complete abusive email trail leading up to Phil's final threat. In his cover letter, the lawyer suggested their next step would be to bring suit for intentional infliction of emotional distress. Dominion finally agreed to a settlement that included monetary damages and reassurances that all future reference requests would be positive.

When the headhunter next submitted Tyler as a candidate, the new company asked for an interview right away and hired him on the spot.

But Phil didn't lose his job at Dominion.

Like the Self-Righteous Narcissist from the last chapter, the Vindictive Narcissist must always be in the right. If you challenge his authority, you are not only in the wrong but you make yourself an enemy. He will go on the attack. If you fight back, he will try to destroy you. As Tyler's lawyer told him, going "mano-a-mano" with a Vindictive Narcissist is a losing proposition. It will lead to an escalating and increasingly vicious battle to prove who is the winner.

A similar scenario plays out in arguments between married couples where one or the other partner is highly narcissistic. For example, every few weeks my client Adam would come to his session in despair following another slash-and-burn fight with his wife, Lili. The dispute would usually begin over some minor issue: Adam's shift ran late and he neglected to call home. Or they went on a bike ride together and he outpaced her. Or he responded with enthusiastic support for her decision to enroll in college courses and she accused him of caring only about money and status.

"You don't think I'm good enough!" she cried.

If Adam defended himself, Lili turned up the volume on her criticism. Caring only about money became "You understand nothing about love. You never have." Forgetting to let her know he'd be working late escalated to "You're so unbelievably selfish! You never think about anyone but yourself!" She accused Adam of deliberately trying to humiliate her by proving he had greater strength and endurance on the bike. "You're so fucking competitive! All you care about is winning!" *Never, always, nothing*: When shame and narcissism color marital spats, the language grows increasingly absolute. "That's not fair; I didn't mean it that way!" Adam often responded, which only caused Lili to escalate even further.

"What a fucking waste, all these years! I want a divorce!"

Following a day or two of bitter silence, Lili would "forget" about their fight and the vicious things she had said. She wouldn't remember telling Adam she wanted a divorce. When he least expected it, he'd receive a loving text message at work, or come home to find that Lili had set the dinner table with candles and flowers. She never made mention of the stony silence but behaved as if she adored him, calling herself the "luckiest girl in the world."

Lili's volatile nature demonstrates many features of Borderline Personality Disorder, but at the same time, she is highly narcissistic and struggles with shame. She'd grown up in a trailer park and had been molested by her grandfather and older brother. She dropped out of high school and married at the age of seventeen because she was pregnant. That first marriage lasted only a few years, ending in a bitter divorce and relentless battles over child support. Adam, by contrast, came from a well-educated, intact family; he had earned an advanced degree and was highly successful in his field.

On an unconscious level, Lili experienced herself as a loser but couldn't bear the agony of shame. Ever on guard against narcissistic injury, she could turn vicious if she felt slighted. When shame threatened to emerge in their marital spats, it ignited the winner-loser dynamic and she experienced Adam as deliberately intending to humiliate her. Once engaged in the battle, she would stop at nothing to win, viciously savaging Adam's sense of self-worth along the way. In other words, through her vindictive behavior, she off-loaded the unbearable feelings of internal defect and damage onto her husband.

Tina Swithin experienced similar fluctuations between being idealized and then eviscerated by her ex-husband, Seth. In the beginning of their relationship he adored her, lavishing her with gifts, flowers, and expensive trips, though she gradually came to understand that he viewed her as inferior. He spoke of his own parents as well educated, superior people with a perfect marriage that had endured for more than thirty years. Tina, on the other hand, had come from a broken family; she'd suffered at the hands of a highly narcissistic mother who eventually killed herself. Tina had not gone to college.

In one of their early fights before they married, Seth turned vicious when she dared to criticize his impulsive behavior. "You are psycho," he told her. "You are white trash."[2] When she didn't back down, he went for the jugular: "You are bipolar just like your mom, and you need help!" The Vindictive Narcissist often knows exactly what will hurt the most. As Swithin describes it, "He said the words that he knew would kill me inside. I would never be like my mom. His words cut me to my core. No one had ever said anything so painful to me."[3] After Swithin broke off their relationship, Seth spent weeks trying to win her back with flowers, cards, and abject apologies by email. He eventually succeeded.

Years later, when she finally decided to divorce him, Seth's behavior became increasingly vindictive. He bombarded her with vicious emails and threatened to spread lies about her supposed promiscuity. One night he left increasingly drunken, angry voice messages when she stopped answering his calls:

> 8am tomorrow morning Saturday I will be emailing 3,000 people every picture that I have of you and ultimately, Tina you will be wrecked in this community. I do not care. I think you are white trash, I think you are a slut. . . .
>
> I will email 3,000 people and show your infidelity and the bottom line Tina is that you are a bad person. . . .
>
> You are a white trash bitch . . . YOU are a LOOSER [sic]. Do you understand this? And I am going to prove it in court. You are a looser, you are white trash, YOU ARE WHITE TRASH, do you understand this?[4]

With a vindictive desire to wound, Seth tried to destroy Tina's self-esteem by making her feel like a loser. Throughout the nasty divorce proceedings and protracted battles over child support and visitation, he savaged her with contempt: "You are a pathetic human being. Worthless. Uneducated."[5]

During their courtship and early months together, Seth had always described himself to Tina as having been the "most popular person in [high] school. He was the captain of every sports team. He was a surfer. All of the girls loved him."[6] In truth, as Swithin later learned from one of Seth's childhood friends, he had actually been "shy, unpopular and socially awkward."[7] The parents whom Seth idealized turned out to have a marriage marked by serial infidelity and discord. Plagued by an unbearable sense of defect and inferiority, Seth created an idealized self-image and became vicious when Tina challenged it. He attempted to destroy her reputation and force her to carry his off-loaded sense of shame: *She* was the contemptible loser.

The Vindictive Narcissist isn't always so blatant; the viciousness can be quite subtle and sometimes invisible to those who don't know the person well. For instance, the ex-husband of my client Winona (discussed in the last chapter) sent a very reasonable-sounding email to selected members of their church, including the pastoral counselors who had tried to help them salvage their marriage, portraying himself as a man of God abandoned by his wife. He then directly impugned Winona's mental sanity while planting doubts about her fitness as a mother, all couched in the language of "concern." He insisted that he still loved his ex-wife and cared only that she get the proper care she so desperately needed.

THE NARCISSIST UNDER ATTACK

As we have seen, Extreme Narcissists create and constantly defend a false self-image in order to escape from shame. In the process, they often ignore, circumvent, or rewrite facts that challenge this image. Sometimes, they merely exaggerate or distort; often they tell outright lies. For the Vindictive Narcissist, the drive to prove oneself a winner and triumph over shame renders the truth irrelevant. As Swithin explains, "Seth lies to re-create his own reality, subsequently allowing himself to escape his inner plagued mind."[8]

Because of his distorted, defensive relationship to reality, the Extreme Narcissist often *believes* the lies he tells, both to himself and to other people. He doesn't see himself as a liar but rather as an embattled defender of the "truth" as he has come to see it. As hard as it may be for most of us to believe, the Extreme Narcissist who lies doesn't always do so in a self-aware way, consciously attempting to disguise the truth. Rather, he tells lies to support a defensive identity he has come to view as synonymous with himself. In other words, the *relentless narcissistic defense* involves a nonstop effort to bolster lies erected against shame, insisting that they reflect the truth.

When those lies are challenged and shame threatens to emerge, the Extreme Narcissist may feel under attack. In less toxic cases, he may react as if he has been the victim of injustice, taking refuge in self-righteous indignation or self-pity. The husband of my client Winona, for example, saw himself as a long-suffering martyr to her supposed mental illness, implicitly asking other people to feel sorry for him. In more dangerous cases, the Vindictive Narcissist may perceive any challenge to his "truth" as a vicious attack and then retaliate in kind. Often the perceived attack results from some unintended slight to the person's self-regard, as in the case of Tyler McOwen, who started off on the wrong foot with his new boss by failing to recognize him. Sometimes, the Vindictive Narcissist will feel attacked by people who simply disagree with him: He must always be *right*, and anyone who argues otherwise becomes an enemy.

One-time vice presidential candidate Sarah Palin has a long history of retaliating against people who dared to oppose her, who disagreed with her, or even those deemed insufficiently supportive of her views. She has also shown a persistent disregard for the truth, prompting Leslie Ridle, a longtime political operative in Alaska, to describe her as a "pathological liar."[9] And many people who have come to know her—including Laura Chase, who ran Palin's first campaign for mayor of Wasilla—have wondered whether she suffers from Narcissistic Personality Disorder.[10]

In a 2004 op-ed piece written for the *Anchorage Daily News* and repeated several times since, Palin famously stated: "All I ever really needed to know I learned on the basketball court." She meant that her involvement in high school sports, more than any other experience, helped to define her later behavior as a politician. While she likes to focus on the values that sports and politics supposedly have in common ("determination and resolve," for example),[11] it is the drive to *win* that truly unites these two arenas of her life.

Palin's high school teammates nicknamed her the "Barracuda" because of her relentless pursuit of victory at all costs, a competitive drive she inherited from her father. Chuck Heath taught science at the junior high school in Wasilla but also served as his daughter's track coach at the high school she attended. Friends from childhood describe Heath as overbearing and hypercompetitive.[12] A longtime Wasilla acquaintance puts it this way: Chuck Heath "had a mean streak, and very high expectations for the kids. . . . And whenever anybody got involved in any sport, they had to win. There was no such thing as losing. Being competitive is one thing, but Chuck carried it way beyond that."[13]

According to Yvonne Bashelier, one of Palin's teammates on the track team under Coach Heath, "winning meant everything to him."[14] Bashelier understands how Palin must have suffered under her father's merciless, bullying methods because she endured them as well. "Sarah *can't lose*. That is her worst fear in life, and that is what her father not only did to her, but me also. Sarah's gone to a dark hole inside herself and I think every move she makes, she hears her father in the background, yelling at her, pushing her, and pushing her."[15]

Palin's mother, Sally, provided little maternal comfort to offset his harshness, mostly because she lost all interest in mothering once she joined the Wasilla Assembly of God. An old family friend says that Sarah and her siblings "were not tended to as children" and that Sally "never really functioned as a mother."[16] Another Wasilla acquaintance says "there was not a lot of tenderness or loving in that household, mostly because Sally never really was a mom. She just wasn't a nurturing person."[17] In *Going Rogue*, Palin tries to paint her childhood as fairly idyllic, a *Father Knows Best* version of American family life, but in truth, she grew up with an unempathic mother and a brutal, hypercompetitive, and dictatorial father.

Chuck Heath wielded political influence in Wasilla, and in order to get his way—that is, to *win*—he demonstrated the same brutal character. When the city council voted unanimously to support the firing of Heath's good friend, the high school principal, he mounted an effort to recall three council members, all women. According to one of those women, Pat O'Hara, Heath "created a lynch mob mentality."[18] He spread rumors that the women were having affairs with the new school superintendent. "The tactics were violent and dangerous," O'Hara recalls. Angry mobs would heckle them after school board meetings, and then "we'd find death threats written in the snow on our cars."[19]

Heath and others "created such a maelstrom that nobody was safe for a while," O'Hara adds. "They were bullies, pure and simple, and essentially that's what Sarah and her cohorts are today."[20]

Bully is a word frequently used by people who have known Sarah

Palin well. Longtime Wasilla resident Zane Henning says that Palin was "standoffish" as a girl, and "if she didn't get her way she was a bully."[21] When author Joe McGinnis moved to Wasilla in 2010 to research his book about Palin, he found many area residents unwilling to speak to him because they feared retaliation by Sarah and her husband, Todd: "More and more I discover that fear of the Palins is endemic throughout the Valley. I hear repeatedly that they've always been bullies."[22] When a handyman came to do some repairs on the house McGinnis had rented next door to the Palins, he arrived with pieces of cardboard duct-taped over the front and rear license plates of his truck. Since moving in next door, McGinnis had become Public Enemy No. 1 as far as the Palins were concerned; the handyman didn't want to become a target for revenge because he'd dared to help him.[23]

Vicious, *vengeful*, and *vindictive* are three other words often used to describe Sarah Palin. After serving on the Wasilla city council for two terms, she decided to challenge the incumbent mayor, John Stein, a man who had supported and nurtured her political career. According to another city council member at the time, she ran a "vicious" campaign against Stein.[24] With the support of her Assembly of God congregation, she mounted a challenge with "brutal" religious undertones. There was a "whisper campaign" that Stein was not a Christian, and because his wife hadn't taken his last name when they married, rumors spread that they were "living in sin."[25]

"Palin had been outraged that several city administrators had openly supported Stein during the election," and after she defeated him, she retaliated by demanding that all of her department heads resign.[26] For Sarah Palin, you are either with her or against her. Because Wasilla Library director Mary Ellen Emmons fought Palin's efforts to ban offending books from the library, Palin tried to fire her. The censorship battle did not play well in Wasilla, and "there were rumblings of a Palin recall movement."[27] An editorial in the *Frontiersman*, Wasilla's local paper, noted that "Palin seems to have assumed that her election was instead a coronation. Welcome to Kingdom Palin, the land of no accountability."[28]

Palin also terminated the employment of Wasilla's chief of police, Irl Stambaugh, because he opposed her positions on bar closing hours and expanded rights for gun owners. Stambaugh was a widely respected man who had once been nominated to be Alaska's Municipal Employee of the Year. When he challenged his dismissal in court, Palin lied "at nearly every turn in the court proceedings" and fabricated a story in which he supposedly tried to seduce her.[29] Stambaugh was outraged that she would apparently say anything to prevail, regardless of its truth.[30]

She also felt entitled to disregard the law. She illegally appointed two friends to fill vacant seats on the city council, until the city attorney informed her that she had no authority to appoint council members. Without obtaining the required council approval, she "used city money to lease a new gold Ford Expedition . . . and took $50,000 that had been budgeted for road improvement and repair and used it to redecorate her office at city hall."[31] When council member Nick Carney informed her that this behavior was against the law, she replied, "I'm the mayor and I can do whatever I want until the courts tell me to stop."[32]

As governor of Alaska, Palin displayed the same traits. She ignored the law and felt entitled to use her office for personal gain rather than public service. She exerted her power to exact revenge against her opponents. And she lied. Nowhere are these traits more evident than in the scandal that eventually came to be known as

Troopergate. When her sister Molly's marriage to state trooper Mike Wooten ended in divorce, Palin spent years trying to get him fired; by divorcing her sister, Wooten had become an enemy. Palin lied under oath about supposedly abusive behavior she had witnessed and then launched a smear campaign to destroy his reputation.

In particular, she pressured her public safety commissioner, Walter Monergan, to fire Wooten. Over eighteen months, there were "some three-dozen interactions . . . initiated by either Palin, her husband, or members of her administration relative to Wooten's status as a trooper."[33] Because he believed that her behavior violated Wooten's rights, Monergan resisted that pressure and she eventually fired him.[34] A later ethics investigation by the bipartisan Alaska Legislative Council concluded that Palin had "abused her power" and that "impermissible pressure was placed on several subordinates in order to advance a personal agenda."[35] In the same vindictive vein, she later fired longtime friend and legislative director John Bitney because he was dating a woman whose former husband happened to be a close friend of Todd Palin's.[36]

Many people who have known the Palins well describe their marriage as an unhappy one, full of conflict and "frequent mutual threats of divorce."[37] Old friends also recall that Todd Palin did most of the parenting and that his wife never took care of their kids. When Todd was away working on the North Slope, one friend recalls, the "kids had to fend for themselves" while "Sarah would be up in her bedroom with the door closed saying she didn't want to be disturbed." Another friend says "she never took care of those kids." They "never had any parenting, they had to raise each other."[38]

In the end, despite the careful image she has cultivated as devoted

"Hockey Mom," Sarah Palin seems to have been a mother much like her own: detached, self-absorbed, and entirely lacking in empathy. Once again, narcissism begets narcissism.

For the Vindictive Narcissist, the winner-loser dynamic involved in competition escalates into warfare. He sees the world in terms of enemies and allies: people who provide uncritical support and admiration are "good"; anyone who challenges him is "bad" and must be annihilated. Tina Swithin's ex-husband, Seth, tried to destroy her reputation by spreading vicious rumors and abusing the court system. Sarah Palin fired government employees who hadn't supported her, launched a vendetta against her former brother-in-law for disrespecting her family, and drummed Irl Stambaugh from office with lies and misrepresentations when he questioned her agenda.

Because the behavior of Vindictive Narcissists is so mean-spirited and vengeful, you might find it almost impossible to empathize with them. They often appear to be so merciless, so cold-blooded in their thirst for revenge that they seem entirely "other," lacking in the softer emotions we associate with being human. It helps to keep the *relentless narcissistic defense* in mind: All Extreme Narcissists are constantly on guard against the experience of shame, and whenever it actually breaks through, they feel flooded with unbearable pain.

In their account of the 2008 presidential election, John Heilemann and Mark Helperin give a poignant account of Palin's state of mind as she prepared for her debate with Joe Biden.[39] The disastrous interview with Katie Couric had destroyed Palin's self-confidence and she had fallen into "a kind of catatonic stupor." She was barely eating, drinking, or sleeping. "When her aides tried to quiz her, she would routinely shut down—chin on her chest, arms folded, eyes cast to the floor, speechless and motionless."[40] Under the "searing scrutiny she was receiving," she lived in constant fear of deeper humiliation.

In this portrait, we see the Vindictive Narcissist in that rare moment when the relentless narcissistic defense has broken down. Overwhelmed with shame and humiliation, she becomes unable to function. Tina Swithin also witnessed this kind of breakdown when Seth's usual defenses failed him. One night when confronted by his brother with the lies he had told about his childhood (portraying himself as popular when he'd actually been shy and withdrawn), Seth seemed wounded and momentarily unable to assert his superiority.[41] Instead, he withdrew into silence and drank heavily for the rest of the evening.

Seth had addictions to several different "drugs"—to exercise and spending as well as to alcohol—and relied upon the high they gave him to reinflate his superior sense of self when threatened by the emergence of core shame. In the next chapter, we'll take a closer look at the relationship between addiction and narcissism, and how the Addictive Narcissist makes use of his drugs to ward off the unconscious experience of internal damage or ugliness.

How to Cope with the Vindictive Narcissist

Because the Vindictive Narcissist is so relentless in the pursuit of revenge and is capable of causing great harm to his enemies, it's crucial not to become a target. As always, do nothing that may wound his self-esteem or make him feel humiliated. Avoid direct conflict and disagreement whenever possible. Even if you feel triggered by his hypercompetitiveness or offended by the lies he tells, do not challenge him head-on. Unfortunately, we usually don't recognize that we're dealing with a Vindictive Narcissist until it's too late and we have already caused offense. In that case, if you can't eliminate or restrict further communication, the best approach is a legalistic one.

Tyler McOwen preserved email exchanges with his boss, kept a detailed log of their interactions, and relied on third-party witnesses to defend himself against Phil's vendetta. Tina Swithin kept a daily calendar-style journal to document her interactions with Seth once divorce proceedings got underway. Like Tyler, she preserved all email and text exchanges. She used GPS tracking software on her daughters' cell phones to determine their whereabouts during Seth's visitations; in this way, she was able to identify lies he told the court about where he had taken them. Most Vindictive Narcissists have perfected the art of the plausible lie, and you will need evidence to expose them.

Be prepared to find yourself painted a villain. In his pursuit of revenge, the Vindictive Narcissist may try to destroy your reputation at work, in your family, or within the community at large. She may tell blatant lies as part of her smear campaign. Though you will of course feel offended, it's important not to retaliate in kind or attempt to turn the tables. If the Vindictive Narcissist feels you have engaged in battle, she will escalate the violence of her assault, stopping at nothing in order to win. Take the high ground and stick to the truth; don't speak ill of your enemy unless you have to. Over time, the Vindictive Narcissist will inevitably reveal her true nature to the people around you, and you will feel vindicated.

Bear in mind that shame is always an issue. While Vindictive Narcissists feel driven to disguise it, from themselves as well as other people, they actually feel frightened, defective, and vulnerable on an unconscious level. By assaulting your sense of self, they strive to make *you* feel that way instead. Whenever she received hostile texts or emails from Seth, Tina Swithin pictured him as "a sad, insecure,

6-year-old bully acting out."[42] Rather than responding defensively, triggered by his nastiness and contempt, she disciplined herself to respond in neutral ways, focusing on the facts. The Vindictive Narcissist continually invites you to reengage in battle; your best response is to decline the invitation and remain civil, factual, and concise.

"MY DRUG MEANS MORE TO ME THAN YOU DO"

The Addicted Narcissist

The psychoanalyst Donald Nathanson tells a personal anecdote to illustrate the relationship between shame and alcohol use. At the age of nineteen, while working on a research project at the Marine Biological Laboratory in Woods Hole, he fell in love for the first time with a beautiful young woman named Elissa. Martin, a colleague at Woods Hole who was "taller, better looking, [and] more 'experienced'" than Nathanson, clearly envied his friend's good fortune in finding so "lovely a companion."[1]

Working late one night, Nathanson dropped by Martin's office and found him "locked in passionate embrace" with Elissa. Nathanson felt deeply humiliated and "was barely able to breathe for the pain that suffused every fiber of my being."[2] He hurried off to his neighborhood tavern, where he

> took an unaccustomed seat at the bar and stared wordlessly at the
> bartender. I have no idea what he saw in my face, but without any

further clue he placed before me a double shot of bourbon, which I swallowed in a gulp. Once again he filled my glass, once again I downed my medicine. Feeling immensely better and not a whit inebriated, I paid up and left without talking to anyone.[3]

Nathanson uses this story to show that "one of the primary actions of alcohol is to release us from the bonds of shame."[4] He explains that other forms of "hedonism"—recreational drugs and casual sex, for example—serve the same purpose.

This method doesn't work as well for what Nathanson calls "chronic enduring shame," however.[5] Alcohol and other drugs help us to weather the occasional blow to our self-esteem without causing much disruption in our lives, but when we are afflicted by shame at our core, we may come to rely upon those drugs for ongoing, continuous relief. A pernicious cycle sets in: We turn to our drug of choice to escape from shame, often using more of it than we intended; once it wears off, we feel even more shame for having abused the drug or "falling off the wagon." Because the compounded shame feels unbearably painful, we once again turn to our drug for release.

Alcoholics refer to this dynamic as the "squirrel cage," where the search for release in alcohol leads to shame and a further need for alcohol in order to relieve it, producing more shame, and so on. John Bradshaw has written extensively about the relationship between shame and various forms of addiction; he believes that shame afflicts everyone who struggles with compulsive or addictive behaviors. Within that group, he includes gamblers, workaholics, sex addicts, and those who struggle with eating disorders.

Addictive and narcissistic personalities have many features in common. This is not to suggest that all addicts are narcissists, but many men and women who struggle with addictive behavior display a pronounced lack of empathy for the people around them. They have a stronger relationship with their drug than they do with their partners, often viewing those significant others as mere "deliverers of supplies."[6] Addicts also rely upon their drugs to boost self-esteem at the expense of the people around them, withdrawing from "the stress of interpersonal relationships into a drug-induced grandiosity . . . and a narcissistic relational style."[7]

An inflated sense of self-importance and a lack of empathy for others.

For many young people, video and online games may function as another kind of addictive drug. In particular, MMORPGs (massively multiplayer online role-playing games) allow the Addicted Narcissist to escape from shame into an alternate reality where he can occupy a fictional identity. At the age of twenty-seven, Ian came to me for help with such an addiction.

"THERE, I'M EVERYTHING I WANT TO BE"

After graduating from college with a degree in computer science, Ian turned down an offer from Google and instead went to work for a small start-up in Silicon Valley, accepting a lower salary in exchange for shares in the company. Several years later the start-up was absorbed by a much larger competitor—not one of those billion-dollar acquisitions that make headlines, but one that left Ian with more than a million dollars in the bank. He quit his job, gave up his small apartment, and moved into a larger rental home with his girlfriend, Concha—a Philippine divorcée in her mid-thirties with two small children. Concha worked at a low-wage job and Ian paid the rent. He was twenty-six years old at the time.

Ian's modest wealth gave him the time and freedom to figure out his next move without the pressure to earn money right away. He knew he wanted to found his own Internet company, but he had no clear vision about which type it would be. He played with different possibilities in the areas of social media and mobile apps but couldn't settle on any one of them. In the meantime, he spent many hours reading about Internet entrepreneurs who had made a fortune. He particularly admired Paul Graham and devoted hours to the study of his essays, as if they were gospel. Like many young men of his age and educational background, he idolized Steve Jobs.

Ian also began playing a popular MMORPG in his free time. This type of game allows millions of players across the globe to enter an artificial world and inhabit an alternate identity or *avatar*. By completing quests, acquiring skills, and battling other characters, a player can rise in power and status within this world. Popular websites post the rankings of various players by the names they have chosen for their avatars; within the MMORPG universe, the most successful of these players become celebrated in forums devoted to the game, admired by thousands of people they have never met.

As the months progressed and Ian couldn't settle on a business plan, he spent more and more time inhabiting his avatar and gradually rose through the rankings. He'd stay awake all night playing the game, have breakfast with Concha and her children in the morning before they left for work or school, then sleep most of the day. Sometimes he awoke with a feeling of dismay that he was wasting his life; he'd swear off the game and try to focus more on his business future, though his resolution never lasted more than a day or two. After several hours of staring blankly at the computer screen, he'd convince himself to log on to the MMORPG world in order to clear his mind. "Just for a half hour or so," he'd tell himself.

Binge playing usually followed. Sometimes he'd play for fifteen to twenty hours on end, logging off only when he could no longer keep his eyes open. Ian's avatar eventually ranked within the top ten worldwide; in a remote, anonymous way, he had become a celebrity. Meanwhile, his relationship with Concha began to suffer. Constantly on the verge of exhaustion, Ian felt virtually no interest in sex. While financially generous toward her children, he had never had much of a relationship with them. Concha subtly pressured him to marry her, but Ian had no intention of doing so. He told himself it was because he eventually wanted biological children of his own and she'd already had a hysterectomy.

It was at this point that Ian contacted me for therapy. During our very first session, he said he believed his difficulties might be shame-based. He'd read extensively in the self-help field and particularly gravitated toward the work of John Bradshaw. He described his parents as anxious, hypercritical people. Throughout childhood, he had felt continuously worried that he would make a mistake and they'd yell at him. Simple infractions, like eating leftovers his mother had been saving for another meal or drinking milk directly from the carton, could provoke a long harangue. They didn't actually punish him; they just made him feel as if he were always doing something wrong.

Ian also described both parents as "obsessive." Simple problems such as how to operate a new cell phone could flood the household with anxiety as they bickered over the instruction manual. These fights could go on for hours, filling Ian with such dread he couldn't bear to be around them. He always felt as if some disaster were in the offing, that the emotional stakes were much higher than seemed to be warranted by their confusion over, say, how to record an outgoing message for voicemail. School offered him a haven from the anxiety-ridden home. He was academically gifted and eventually went to a top university on scholarship.

In one of our early sessions, Ian also told me about a slight physical abnormality that troubled him. He'd been born with a cleft upper lip that had been surgically corrected during infancy, leaving a scarcely detectable scar. In our sessions, I'd had a vague awareness that something was slightly different about his upper lip, but I didn't fully notice the scar until Ian drew it to my attention. He told me that in social situations, he became quite self-conscious about the scar and worried that people found him unattractive because of it. Though he was actually attractive in a wholesome, all-American sort of way, he often felt ugly.

Our early sessions focused on the core shame, sometimes confused with physical ugliness, that had afflicted Ian throughout life. He'd always felt out of synch with his peers, as if there were something a bit "off" about him. When new friends came over to his home, he felt ashamed of his parents and their obvious dysfunction—the way they would anxiously bicker in front of total strangers or yell at him over nothing. We talked about his deep sense that something had gone wrong in his development, leaving him convinced that he was fundamentally deformed or defective, and his fear that there was something fraudulent about his entire life. He may have had money in the bank, a girlfriend, and two children living in his home, but it all felt fake—the illusion of "normal."

When Ian talked about his plan to launch an Internet start-up, his grandiosity became clear. In the future he envisioned, he saw himself as an innovator on the same level as Steve Jobs. He intended to build a new company and eventually launch an IPO that would earn him billions of dollars, placing him alongside Sergey Brin and Jeff Bezos in the pantheon of Internet entrepreneurs. Nothing less would do. In our work together, we focused on the link between the grandiose imaginary self detached from reality, and the feeling of core shame that had always plagued him.

Over time, Ian made some headway in developing a more realistic business plan. He settled on a platform that would match prospective interns with companies offering placements, linking the student database from his alma mater to businesses in the area with internships to fill. This was to be a kind of pilot project to attract angel investors, with a planned expansion to many different campuses and corporations nationwide. None of the technical issues involved in building such a platform posed a major challenge. Ian was a crack coder and worked well in isolation.

Troubles began to arise when it came time to hire people. Conventional wisdom in the start-up world holds that you need a co-founder in order to launch a successful enterprise, and the idea of interviewing prospects for that position filled Ian with dread. He felt confident in his ability to tackle just about any technical challenge, but shame and self-doubt always surfaced in his relationships with other people, particularly strangers. When interviewing a prospect, he came across as insecure and lacking in focus. He constantly second-guessed himself and questioned his own judgment. Like his parents, he would obsess about small details.

Ian's anxieties eventually became so intense that he began canceling scheduled interviews, often calling a candidate less than an hour before their designated time, claiming illness or a business crisis that demanded his immediate attention. With some candidates, he rescheduled their interviews so many times that they eventually lost interest. Filled with shame and a sense of failure when he canceled, Ian would withdraw into the universe of Internet gaming. When his shame was particularly intense, the retreat lasted days. He missed many of our sessions during this period because he couldn't bear to confront his shame, often playing the MMORPG straight through our appointment time without even realizing he had forgotten it.

Concha finally came to the conclusion that Ian would never marry her and decided to break off their relationship. She and her children moved out. Entirely alone now in his rental home, Ian withdrew more deeply into the world of online gaming. The shame he felt had driven him into a fantasy world, where he could successfully battle challengers and build his online reputation; but as a result, he felt even more shame, which further fueled his addiction to the game, and so on. In our work together, we referred to this as the "downward shame spiral." During the worst of these bouts, Ian quit therapy, largely because he couldn't bear to face me or his shame. I didn't hear from him for many months.

Eventually, he reached out again and we resumed our work. Over time, within the context of a psychotherapy relationship in which he felt understood and accepted, Ian learned to weather these shame attacks. If he happened to succumb, he emerged more quickly from his fantasy world. As he gradually built his company and identified a co-founder, he also built self-confidence. Ian replaced the downward shame spiral with a virtuous cycle where real achievement led to self-respect, which then enabled him to accomplish even more, building more confidence, et cetera.

SELF-ESTEEM AND THE CRIPPLING POWER OF SHAME

Most of the Extreme Narcissists described so far crave the spotlight and often accomplish a great deal in order to demonstrate that they are winners. Others retreat into a fantasy world instead—like my client Nicole, who viewed herself as a secret musical genius but lacked basic skills; or like Shiloh, who had shown such promise as a child but never achieved full financial independence from his parents. In flight from shame, Ian became a kind of hero to his many online fans while stagnating in his personal life; a grandiose self-image as the next Steve Jobs rescued him from shame but often blocked him from making step-by-step progress toward a realistic goal.

Ian's MMORPG alter ego represented a kind of *idealized false self* that helped him evade the shame-ridden, damaged self at his core. All Extreme Narcissists harbor a grandiose self-image that serves the same purpose: Whether they seek to confirm it via their outsized ambition, or try to shore it up in a secret fantasy life, they are all in flight from shame. I find James Cameron's 2009 film *Avatar* to be a useful metaphor for this psychological process.

At the opening of the movie, Jake Sully has suffered a severe spinal cord injury that leaves him a paraplegic. An operation to repair the damage is beyond his financial means, and so in order to earn the money, Jake volunteers for a specialized military mission to the planet Pandora. Through the miracle of medical technology, he learns to psychically link with and inhabit an avatar or alternative physical self on that planet. In contrast to his damaged, paraplegic self, this avatar is healthy, fit, and stands ten feet tall, with enormous physical prowess and sensory capabilities. Embodying this avatar allows Jake to not only escape his damaged body (at least temporarily) but also to surpass his human potential. His experience on Pandora ultimately proves to be more real, more meaningful to him than his actual life: At the movie's end, he finds a way to transcend his human physical damage and move permanently to the realm of his superior Na'vi self.

Like Jake Sully, the Addicted Narcissist finds the experience of his drug-altered consciousness to be more compelling than "real life." While it may not be apparent to those on the outside, the addict often feels quite grandiose while under the influence—a fact frequently discussed by professionals who treat and write about addiction. Alcoholics Anonymous "has long recognized that the alcoholic's grandiosity . . . and lack of humility are the most important obstacles" to his recovery.[8] For the alcoholic and other addicts, their relation to their drugs embodies a *narcissistic defense* wherein "a false self or grandiose self . . . guards against painful feelings of shame and low self-worth."[9]

As Heinz Kohut explains, it "is the lack of self-esteem [and] the dreadful feeling of the fragmentation of the self that the addict tries to counteract by his addictive behavior."[10] Kohut includes overeating and promiscuous sexuality as additional examples of addiction. The so-called sex addict may resort to pornography as a way of counteracting feelings of shame—my client Jason, for example, who visited XXX websites and masturbated compulsively. He may also use hook-up apps for casual sex or employ prostitutes. For such men (and they are largely male), orgasm is a self-administered drug that temporarily relieves their shame—the "dreadful feeling" of a self that is damaged and in pieces.

In the 2011 film aptly titled *Shame*, the main character, Brandon, is a sex addict who masturbates compulsively, in rest room stalls at work and after viewing pornography at home in his austere apartment. He has several orgasms a day, none of which gives him any real pleasure. He also brings home women from bars and hires prostitutes on a regular basis. Brandon leads a life of almost complete emotional isolation. He doesn't want authentic connection with other people and lacks empathy for everyone he knows, including his sister, Sissy. Instead, he uses people in a druglike fashion to alleviate pain. Although we never learn the exact details, the film makes clear that Brandon and Sissy shared a traumatic childhood that damaged them both. Masturbation or indiscriminate sex offers brief relief from shame but results in even more shame that then needs relief, et cetera—the sexual equivalent of the alcoholic's squirrel cage.

Many years ago, back when Internet chat rooms and bulletin boards were heating up, my client David became obsessed with the world of online "relationships." A short, slightly overweight, and physically unexceptional man in his mid-thirties, David struggled with profound shame. His family background was deeply troubled: During his late teens, his mother had committed suicide and he dropped out of college not long after her death. His older sister was anorexic. He had never managed to find and apply himself to any meaningful career, spending most of his adult life either supported by his father and stepmother or working in low-level retail jobs.

Despite a deep longing for connection, David had never managed to develop a relationship of any duration. Instead, he tended to become fixated upon unattainable men, extremely attractive and successful members of the "A Gay" social world, as he called it. As far as I could tell from his accounts, these men appeared to be Seductive Narcissists who used their charisma to exploit David without reciprocating his desire for sex. Though frustrated in his physical longings, David nonetheless felt better about himself by being in their orbit, as if association with such superiority made him special.

Often he developed subservient relationships with these men. He'd try to win their love and affection by "doing" for them, regularly canceling his plans when one of his idols called upon him for a favor. For example, he once gave up tickets for a concert he'd been anticipating for months when Neal, a handsome and successful designer, asked him to man his booth at a trade show. Over time, David would grow resentful as he began to realize these men were exploiting him. Eventually there would be an explosive confrontation that ended the friendship. David was a deeply unhappy and lonely man.

When he discovered Internet chat rooms, he found a way to become (at least in fantasy) the person he'd always longed to be. As I believe is often the case in anonymous online "relationships," he completely misrepresented himself. The Online David was younger, taller, and thinner than the real one. He had a dynamic career and drove a different car, owned his own home, et cetera. In other words, Online David had it all and came across as a winner.

His online contacts with strangers often progressed to masturbation and mutual sex talk, either online or over the phone. Although orgasm as shame-relief was the primary goal, David sometimes took pleasure in "meeting" these strangers and getting to know them through hours-long telephone calls during which he continued to misrepresent himself. They'd eventually make plans to get together, but David would always reschedule at the last moment and put off the meeting as long as possible. Eventually he'd either stop returning phone calls and disappear from the other man's life or make a shamed confession and beg off.

David was burdened with profound and intolerable shame. Because he couldn't face that shame and how he felt about his damage, he found authentic relationships impossible. Instead, he took flight from ugly, damaged David into Online David the Winner. Like Jake Sully, he left his damaged self behind and escaped into his ideal new self, using fantasy role-playing and orgasmic pleasure as a kind of self-medication. All Addicted Narcissists use their drug of choice in the same way, to provide relief from a shame-ridden, damaged, or "ugly" self.

In recent years, the media have begun to focus on the growing problem of addiction to plastic surgery. Toby Sheldon, a thirty-three-year-old man profiled on the daytime TV show *The Doctors*, has spent more than $100,000 for surgery to make himself more closely resemble teen idol Justin Bieber, whose youth, fame, and good looks he envies. As profiled on British television, flight attendant Rodrigo Alves has spent more than £100,000 and undergone no fewer than twenty cosmetic procedures including nose jobs, liposuction, six-pack and pec implants, calf shaping, and Botox fillers.[11] He apparently wants to resemble the Ken doll, Barbie's boyfriend, because the toy looks like the ideal man. "With Ken," Alves says, "everything is exactly in the right place, his back, his biceps, his jawline. So of course I'd like to look like him. He's perfect!" Although one of his latest procedures nearly killed Alves, he remains committed to surgically altering his appearance. "I'd like to make my shoulders bigger," he says, "my bum rounder, my pecs larger and probably another nose job."[12]

Alves began this "quest for perfection" with his first nose job at the age of twenty because he'd been teased about its size throughout childhood. "I hated my nose so much and when the swelling went down I was delighted with the results. From that moment on I was

215

hooked." Pop icon Michael Jackson also hated his nose and underwent numerous procedures to alter its shape. He relied on plastic surgery to mold his face into a kind of ideal, returning again and again to the surgeon for further relief from the shame that plagued him.

THE MAN IN THE MIRROR

Either you're a winner in this life, or a loser.
And none of my kids are gonna be losers.[13]
—Joseph Jackson, Michael's father

Michael Joseph Jackson, the ninth of eleven children born to Katherine and Joseph Jackson, began life in poverty and experienced such cruel treatment at the hands of his father that it scarred him for life. To be slapped, spanked, shoved, or even locked in the closet was a daily occurrence. After one of those spankings, when Michael was only three, he threw a shoe at his father in pain and anger. According to brother Marlon, Joseph was so infuriated that he picked Michael up by one leg, held him upside down, and "pummeled him over and over again with his hand, hitting him on his back and buttocks."

"Put him down, Joseph," Katherine screamed. "You're gonna kill him! You're gonna kill him."[14]

During the next few years, as Joseph groomed his sons for stardom, he conducted twice-daily rehearsals under the same brutal regimen. He "brandished a belt and bellowed at them constantly, smacking his sons on their backsides or throwing them into walls if they made a mistake."[15] Even after they had achieved fame and moved into the large family compound on Hayvenhurst Avenue in Encino, Joseph continued to "discipline" his children in a way that became increasingly "ritualized and sadistic. He would make you strip naked first, Michael remembered, then slather you with baby oil before bringing out the cut-off cord from a steam iron . . . and crack it across the back of your thighs, so that when the tip struck it felt like an electric shock."[16]

Michael was so afraid of his father that he would often faint or retch whenever he came into the room.

As he moved into puberty, Michael became increasingly ashamed of his appearance. He had a darker complexion than any of his siblings, to begin with, and his skin had broken out badly during adolescence. He was painfully shy. "When he was onstage, performing, he could transform himself into the desirable person of his dreams: a sexy, outgoing, confident person who exerted total control over himself and his audience. But offstage was another story. When he looked in the mirror, he saw a person he didn't like very much, a person who still allowed himself to be controlled by other people."[17]

Since the age of thirteen, he had also "been fixated on the size of his nose, and his brothers had only made matters worse with their nickname for him: Big Nose. Wide, flat noses were a Jackson family trait, inherited from Joseph."[18] Michael had been contemplating rhinoplasty for years; but in 1979, when he broke his nose during a rehearsal, he finally underwent the first of many such operations. It didn't solve the underlying confidence problem, but he kept altering his face with further operations. He had the surgeon insert a cleft in his chin. He altered the shape of his eyes and mouth. He bleached his skin with Porcelana and other pigment lighteners.

Meanwhile, he was lonely, socially awkward, and miserable. The only time he felt remotely happy was when he was onstage. During an interview with J. Randy Taraborrelli, a staff writer for *Soul* magazine (and later his biographer), Jackson told him, "I'm addicted to the stage. When I can't get on to a stage for a long time, I have fits and get crazy. . . . It's like a part of me is missin' and I gotta get it back, 'cause if I don't, I won't be complete."

Jackson explained that he didn't feel comfortable around "normal people," but when onstage, he opened up and felt as if he had no problems. "Whatever is happening in my life doesn't matter. I'm up there and cuttin' loose and I say to myself, 'This is it. *This* is home. This is exactly where I'm supposed to be, where God meant for me to be.' I am *unlimited* when I'm onstage. I'm number one. But when I'm off the stage, I'm not really . . . happy."[19]

Joseph forbade all of his children to have friends outside the family, and once he became famous, Michael feared that other people only wanted to exploit him. Instead of actual friends, he kept a menagerie of animals at the house on Hayvenhurst—swans, peacocks, llamas, et cetera. He built a small amusement park as well, precursor to the much larger one he would build at Neverland, and filled it with puppet characters. "These are just like real people," Michael explained to Taraborrelli. "Except they don't grab at you or ask you for favours. I feel comfortable with these figures. They are my personal friends."[20] In his bedroom, he kept five female mannequins of different ethnic groups, life-sized and dressed like fashion models. He thought of these mannequins as his friends as well.[21]

He seemed incapable of intimacy with adults his own age. He married Lisa Marie Presley in May of 1994, but as early as December of that year, "London tabloids began reporting that Michael planned to file for divorce after complaining that his wife was 'invading his space.'"[22] Most of the time, Lisa Marie had no idea where to find him and often learned his whereabouts by reading the newspapers. Many people who knew them well—including Michael's longtime PR chief Bob Jones—believed the marriage was nothing more than a publicity stunt.[23] When he later married Debbie Rowe, the mother of two of his children, they never slept in the same bed or even lived together in the same house. They divorced after two years.

Michael Jackson was notoriously fond of children, of course, but most people who knew him well felt that his "relationships" with young boys actually represented an attempt to relive his own lost childhood rather than genuine closeness. He tended to idealize children as innocent and uncorrupted by cynical adults. He became infatuated with one after another, inviting them to Neverland, taking them on tour, buying them extravagant gifts, et cetera. But he also moved on easily whenever he found a new "friend." Gavin Arvizo, the boy whose claims of molestation led to the infamous 2005 trial in California, was deeply hurt when Michael stopped returning his calls and dropped him, long before his family brought the charges.

As his first wife pointed out, Michael's insistence that he loved "all the children of the world" disguised an extreme form of selfishness.[24] When Lisa Marie complained about his decision to take the young Cascio brothers on vacation with him to France—without including her—Michael replied, "What I do is none of your business." He liked to play the benevolent father who showered his "children" with love in the form of extravagant gifts and an opulent, restriction-free lifestyle, but he behaved with a callous disregard for the feelings of his wife, his friends, and his longtime allies and supporters. "When Michael was unhappy with a person, that person was usually ousted from his world. Many important people had shown up in his life and then been banished from it over the years. Some of them, like [his lawyer] John Branca, had considered themselves long-time friends of Michael's, but such status did not save them from being terminated."[25]

Brought up in a world of wealth and privilege from an early age, recognized as the King of Pop and idolized by millions, Michael displayed a sense of entitlement on a grandiose scale. According to Al Malnik, one of the lawyers who tried to help Jackson tame his spending habits, "For Michael it was whatever he wanted, at the time he wanted."[26] Even on the verge of bankruptcy, he would continue to travel with a large entourage, taking over entire hotels for as much as $80,000 per night. According to another of Michael's discarded advisors, "When he didn't get what he wanted, he acted like a spoiled, little kid. He threw temper tantrums. He cried."[27]

"Shopping and spending had become for Michael as addictive as any opiate. Those who worked for him described seeing Jackson leaf through a magazine and order every single product advertised in it."[28] He spent lavishly on antiques, cars, and travel—with an annual budget of $12 million for the latter category alone. For more than a decade, his annual income had averaged $25 million but he still managed to spend between $10 million and $15 million more than he earned.[29] In later years, when on the verge of bankruptcy, he had to live on a relatively austere budget that put his accustomed shopping excursions out of the question; he found the experience "nearly unbearable," as if he were being deprived of a drug.[30]

Even making allowance for his superstar status, Jackson displayed a remarkably grandiose sense of self. Throughout the main house at Neverland were life-sized paintings of Michael. "Nearly every one showed him striking a heroic pose while costumed in brightly colored but vaguely military uniforms that suggested the dandified garb of nineteenth-century European royalty, replete with cape, sword, ruffled collar, and, very often, a crown."[31] Above his bed hung a Last Supper painting that depicted him "sitting at the center of a long table flanked by Walt Disney on one side and Albert Einstein on the other, with Thomas Edison, Charlie Chaplin, Elvis Presley, John F. Kennedy, Abraham Lincoln, and Little Richard" around him.[32]

Although Michael began life as a Jehovah's Witness and for many years avoided all drugs and alcohol, he eventually became addicted to prescription painkillers that he began using following injuries sustained to his scalp during the filming of a Pepsi commercial. Prior to the Jordan Chandler charges surfacing in 1993, "he had made an effort to not over-medicate during recovery from plastic surgeries, explaining to doctors that he wanted to remain 'sharp' for the purpose of making sound business and career decisions."[33] But amidst the allegations of sexual abuse and a humiliating public scandal, Michael became increasingly anxious and unable to sleep. He began to take ever-larger doses of "Percodan, Demerol and codeine, as well as the tranquillizers Valium, Xanax and Ativan."[34] Eventually, he became entirely dependent on these drugs.

For many years, he spent more than $10,000 a month to sustain his addictions. He traveled with a suitcase full of drugs, needles, and IV lines. His "self-medication became so sophisticated . . . over time that the IV lines he used were filled not with a single prescription drug but with combinations of opioids, benzos, and sleeping aids."[35] After several unsuccessful bouts in rehab, he eventually came clean without rehab in the early 2000s; he seemed to be regaining some career momentum when the devastating Martin Bashir documentary *Living with Michael Jackson* aired in 2003. He quickly relapsed. Humiliating exposure in the press and mainstream media fueled a shame-driven retreat into drugs that lasted until his death in June 2009 from an overdose.

Because the disease model of mental health largely eschews psychological explanations, most people have learned to view addiction as a problem of physiological dependence rather than a defensive response to shame. The professional literature regularly focuses on the link between shame and addiction but often gets it backward. Treatment programs help addicts to cope with the shame they feel *as a result* of their addiction but don't usually address the lifelong shame that preceded and induced their addiction. Yes, the addict feels ashamed of his addiction and the self-destructive behavior it causes, but, like Michael Jackson, he originally turned to his drug of choice in order to escape from core shame.

Aided by immense fame and wealth, Jackson made a public display of his grandiosity, driven by ambition to become a number-one winner, the biggest and wealthiest star in show business.[36] Along the way, he became addicted to plastic surgery, spending, public performance, and prescription drugs. To escape from shame, my client Ian withdrew into a private fantasy world of his MMORPG, in which he gained renown within the gaming universe. Along the way, both men showed little concern for the feelings of other people and were almost entirely lacking in empathy for those they supposedly cared about.

How to Cope with the Addicted Narcissist

If you're emotionally involved with an Addicted Narcissist, you need first of all to recognize that you can't possibly "save" him on your own. If you find yourself preoccupied with rescuing the addict, covering for his behavior or bearing the adverse consequences in his place, then you may be engaged in a co-dependent relationship. Like *addiction,* the word *co-dependent* has become so overgeneralized that just about everyone meets the definition. In its original, more limited sense as an outgrowth of Alcoholics Anonymous, co-dependency refers to unhealthy relationships where one person's help tends to support or enable the other person's addictive behavior in subtle, unacknowledged ways.

Appearances to the contrary, the co-dependent personality often satisfies important needs of her own in the course of caretaking. She may *appear* selfless and devoted to the cause of rescue, but in the course of enabling the addict, she comes to feel competent and needed, thereby boosting her self-esteem. The co-dependent may also avoid her own needs by assigning them to the addicted partner. Although it may not be readily apparent, the co-dependent is no more capable of true, mature intimacy than the addict. Co-dependency is not the same thing as interdependency—the universal human condition.

Even more than the other Extreme Narcissists profiled in this book, the Addicted Narcissist forces us to examine ourselves, to question what binds us to a relationship that seems, on the surface, so unsatisfactory. Perhaps the addict's dependency makes you feel secretly superior, like a comparative winner. Maybe your apparent loving devotion and self-sacrifice don't reflect true concern. In other words, your own grandiosity and lack of empathy may be disguised behind a show of saintliness or victimhood. Within the professional literature, *covert narcissist*, *co-narcissist*, and *inverted narcissist* are frequent synonyms for *co-dependent*.

Despite certain conceptual limitations of the twelve-step programs, they are enormously helpful for alcoholics and other addicts, along with co-dependents in recovery. Whether or not they recognize its origins, these programs do acknowledge the role of shame in the maintenance of addictive behavior. By guiding alcoholics through the twelve steps, AA helps them to confront shame within a supportive environment. In lifelong flight from shame, after years of destructive behavior that has only deepened his shame, the addict can rarely confront himself without organizational and professional help.

Intensive psychotherapy is also indicated—if you can persuade the Addicted Narcissist to get it. When the drug of choice poses a substantial threat to his physical health, he may be forced to admit he has a problem. But like other Extreme Narcissists, he may persist in a state of denial for years, especially when the world around him supports his grandiosity and doesn't challenge his callous disregard for the feelings of others.

11

"I'M DIFFICULT BUT NOT IMPOSSIBLE TO MANAGE"

Coping with the Narcissist You Know

The theme of winners vs losers has run throughout this book, focusing on the various ways that an Extreme Narcissist boosts his self-esteem and proves himself a winner at the expense of someone else. A firm grasp of this dynamic will be your single most important tool in coping with the narcissist you know. Seen from a distance, the Extreme Narcissist may appear simply grandiose or arrogant, possibly amusing in his exaggerated self-importance; once you draw nearer and are pulled into his emotional orbit, he'll inevitably involve you in the psychological game of *who's up and who's down*.

What makes the Extreme Narcissist such an enormous challenge is his powerful effect on your self-esteem. The Seductive Narcissist can make you feel grand, elated, and lucky, as if you're a winner—while most of the other types profiled in this book will do everything they can to make you feel like a loser. In other words, when it comes to the narcissist you know, you'll find it hard to be neutral and objective in response to his behavior because he affects your sense of your own value. This is especially true if your self-esteem is fragile and you already tend to see the world in terms of winners and losers—that is, if you have your own shame issues.

In her excellent book on narcissism, social worker Sandy Hotchkiss explains that when you interact "with these individuals, their distortions of reality can cause you to question yourself and doubt your own perceptions."[1] Because they emanate a supreme self-confidence and conviction that they are right, Extreme Narcissists often convince you that you must be wrong, even when you know better. Your relationship with the narcissist you know will sometimes remind you of Alice going down the rabbit hole: You may feel bewildered, on shaky ground when it comes to your own self-perceptions (too big or too small), and unsure about what is or isn't real.

If you're romantically involved with a Seductive Narcissist, your judgment may become clouded by the intoxication of idealized love. Under the influence of this romance drug, you're easily manipulated and prone to make ill-considered choices. Men who fell under my client Julia's spell, for example (see Chapter Five), often spent more money than they had intended; without knowing her well, they pushed for an early relationship commitment because of the way she made them feel about themselves. If you have a history of falling quickly and disastrously in love, this may be your issue. Instead of paying attention to the danger signs, you may disregard them in an effort to sustain or regain a state of bliss.

Tina Swithin's book is full of the Red Flag Warnings she disregarded because Seth often made her feel so incredibly special and deserving—like a winner—and lucky to have found a modern-day Prince Charming. For months, as her relationship troubles mounted, she tried to recapture the lost state of romantic intoxication when she should have walked away long before she married Seth and they had children. Most of the people who became romantically involved with Madonna could have predicted that they would end up discarded like her previous romantic partners, but her charismatic pull and their desire to take part in such glamorous power overrode common sense.

If we struggle with shame, we may be drawn to the Extreme Narcissist because of "the special way they make us feel when we are included in their grandiosity. . . . If being part of their lives makes our own seem fuller or more exciting, we may choose to pay the price or deny that there even is one. When this happens, we may end up sacrificing ourselves to an illusion that leaves us ultimately empty and bruised."[2] My client David (described in the last chapter) repeatedly pursued this type of relationship. He subjugated himself in order to take part in the superior lives of his idols. In flight from his own shame, David ignored the obvious signs of exploitation so he could feel that he belonged within that winner's circle, the "A Gay" world.

Coping with the narcissist you know sometimes means confronting your own shame. If you find yourself continually drawn to or seduced by people because being with them makes you feel special, you may be in flight from core shame and a lifelong sense of unworthiness. This will be especially true for those of us who grew up with a Narcissistic Parent. Sadly, the children of such parents are especially liable to exploitation by the Seductive Narcissist. We may struggle with feelings of never being good enough, and "[when] someone like our narcissistic parent comes along and smiles on us, [we may] respond to this unconsciously as an opportunity for healing."[3]

My client Winona (see Chapter Eight) had grown up with an entirely self-absorbed mother incapable of concern or empathy who looked the other way when a family friend began sexually abusing Winona. Because she was dependent upon her friend for practical and sometimes financial assistance, this Narcissistic Parent traded her own daughter for personal gain. Winona then went on to marry an Extreme Narcissist who forced her to have sex according to a fixed schedule, regardless of her own desires. For years, she complied and tried hard to make her husband, Mark, happy, in the unconscious belief that winning his love and approval would "cure" her lifelong feelings of unworthiness.

In such cases, coping with the narcissist you know means disengaging and turning inward. Winona finally left Mark, filed for divorce, and began individual therapy. As David's treatment progressed, he became much less other-focused and more attuned to his profound feelings of shame. He learned to resist the seductive pull of these men, make better choices in his relationships, and take realistic action to build self-esteem. Sandy Hotchkiss likens this process to "saying no to a drug dependency."[4] A relationship that might make you feel good in the short term actually stands in the way of developing authentic self-esteem.

In short, coping with the narcissist you know begins with self-awareness.

SET LIMITS

Managing the Narcissistic Parent presents a special challenge. Even people who have been grossly mistreated by their mother and father often feel the pressure of filial obligation. As we grow up, we receive repeated social messages that all children should honor their parents. *Feel grateful,* we are told, so we develop a strong sense of duty, even when we have been envied, ignored, or abused. Attempts to explain such hurtful behavior to friends are often met with sentimental bromides: "She's your mother, and down deep, I know she loves you." Without support from friends, family, or society at large, we may doubt the lessons of our own experience.

In addition, the Narcissistic Parent who views her child as a possession or extension of herself feels *entitled* to receive love and respect she hasn't earned. Mora's mother (see Chapter Four) had never shown the smallest sign of maternal love and concern but nonetheless expected Mora to live up to her filial obligations, to shower her with gifts on her birthday, to feel *grateful*. Like many children of Narcissistic Parents, Mora blamed herself for her mother's deficiencies; on a profound level, Mora believed that she must be essentially unlovable.

Though she had learned to keep her distance, my client Winona often told me how guilty she felt for not visiting her mother more often. She sometimes wondered aloud if her childhood had really been "all that bad"; perhaps she had exaggerated the painful parts, ignoring the ways her mother had come through for her. From time to time, she would convince herself she needed to try harder in order to make the relationship work and would schedule a visit. These brutal encounters, full of her mother's anger and recriminations, always left Winona feeling shattered.

In my experience, men and women like Winona often nourish an unconscious hope that the Narcissistic Parent will eventually turn out to be a truly loving mother or father, if only they, the grown children, behave in the right way. *Coping with the Narcissistic Parent begins with giving up hope and grieving for the mother or father you will never have.* You may need professional help to go through this process. It is a sad and deeply painful realization to accept that childhood has passed and you missed your one and only chance to be parented in the ordinary, expected way. You'll have to face your own feelings of shame and unworthiness, too, the inevitable residue of a childhood without love. It's a difficult challenge to face alone.

On a practical level, coping with a Narcissistic Parent involves setting limits to minimize further abuse. Sometimes it means completely breaking off contact. In response to the "Narcissistic Mother" blog post I wrote, I heard from readers who refused to see or communicate with their mothers under any circumstances. Others confined themselves to brief holiday visits and telephone calls on a birthday or anniversary. If you are the son or daughter of Narcissistic Parents, you'll need to develop a parental concern for yourself, so to speak, and shield yourself from more pain. Ignore the social messaging that says mothers *always* love their children; validate your own perceptions and take care of yourself. You deserve better.

If you have a Narcissistic Parent who idealizes you, it may be harder to recognize that a problem exists. Parents normally take pride in their children's achievements, so the exaggerated praise you receive might seem like a form of love. It's difficult, and probably painful, to realize that it isn't really about you. This type of Narcissistic Parent views a child as an idealized extension of himself, the fulfillment of his own winner self-image. Celine's apparently devoted mother (see Chapter Four) exploited her daughter in this way, forcing Celine to enter childhood beauty pageants, study piano, et cetera, all to make her daughter into a winner. Earl Woods exploited Tiger in a similar fashion. Although they may not have been abused, like Mora, these children received parenting that lacked true love and concern.

Facing the truth about a Narcissistic Parent who idealizes you also involves mourning. Coping effectively means, again, setting limits to protect yourself. At some point, it will involve facing the shame that inevitably results from narcissistic parenting.

RESIST THE URGE TO RETALIATE

Even if you grew up with good-enough parents, an Extreme Narcissist may have a powerful effect on your sense of self, exalting you with idealization or wounding you with disdain. None of us is entirely immune: Because we're social animals, defining and expressing ourselves in relation to one another, our self-esteem depends to a significant degree on how others regard us. When they wield power in our lives—at the workplace but also within our families and social lives—Extreme Narcissists may assault our sense of self so brutally that, on an unconscious and sometimes conscious level, our very survival feels at risk. As with any life-threatening attack, we will defend ourselves.

If the narcissist you know regularly wounds your self-esteem, making you feel like a loser, you may respond in ways that embody the narcissistic defenses against shame I've described in preceding chapters. When on the receiving end of contempt, you may protect yourself with righteous indignation, as if you've been treated unfairly and without justification. You may retreat to a stance of wounded innocence and hurl criticisms from behind your defensive wall. In the face of scorn and blame, you may try to turn the tables and reverse the blame. In short, unless you're conscious of the winner-loser dynamic, you may become trapped on a battlefield where you feel compelled to return narcissistic attacks on your character in kind, responding to contempt with contempt, blame with blame.

We're all narcissistic to some degree. Like Natalie, the legal assistant from Chapter Two, you may occasionally protect yourself against the pain of narcissistic injury by shifting blame onto someone else, becoming angry and indignant because you feel treated unjustly, or adopting a stance of superiority and contempt. These are common (and not necessarily pathological) ways in which people react when their self-esteem has been wounded. Most of the time, these are temporary responses. As you cool down, you might be able to see the other person's point of view and accept responsibility where you need to. You might feel remorse for the nasty things you said in the heat of the moment. If your sense of self is strong enough to withstand a blow to your self-esteem, you might even apologize!

If you struggle with shame, however, you may instead become mired in the narcissistic battle of winners vs losers. You may find it difficult to disengage because your self-esteem is on the line: You're too invested in proving that you are right and the other person wrong. Many unhealthy relationships continue this way for years, each side vying bitterly to come out on top and "prove" that the other person is the contemptible, shame-ridden loser. For years, my client Denise and her husband, Eric (see Chapter Eight), engaged in this type of argument; only when both stepped back from the winner-loser confrontation to deal with personal shame did they learn a much healthier approach to conflict.

If this description reminds you of arguments in your relationship, focus on your own narcissistic vulnerabilities instead of assigning blame; next time around, "resist the urge to retaliate."[5] Once you understand this winner-loser dynamic, "don't try to challenge or enlighten" the narcissist you know. He will likely experience your explanations as a form of condescension, leading him to escalate his attacks to escape from impending shame. Instead, "you need to find a way to detach from the feeling of diminishment the narcissist evokes in you" without expecting him to validate your point of view.[6]

CULTIVATE COMPASSION—TO A POINT

In the later stages of her divorce from Seth, Tina Swithin found it useful to think of him as a child throwing a temper tantrum. It helped her cope with his irrational and often brutal attacks to see him as a frightened little boy full of shame. As part of their guidance for dealing with narcissists, many books on the subject suggest adopting a similar perspective. Social worker Wendy Behary offers a detailed description you may find useful:

> Putting yourself in the narcissist's shoes means trying to sense and genuinely feel his inner world. Specific techniques can help you do this. For example, when the narcissist begins to address you sharply, you could superimpose the face of a lonely and unloved little boy over that of the grown man before you. As you picture the face of that child, try to imagine his experience: his painful feelings, his sense of defectiveness and shame, his loneliness and emotional emptiness, the impossible but inescapable conditions he had to meet to gain attention, love, or approval. . . . You summon up your empathy and embrace the boy that the man before you cannot bear to consciously feel.[7]

I realize that the advice to feel compassion for another person while you are under attack sounds like a very tall order, especially since he is most likely incapable of reciprocating your concern. But finding a way to *humanize* the narcissist you know, rather than regarding him as an irrational monster, will help you to salvage your own self-respect and avoid threatening his self-esteem any further.

Most of the profiles, clinical vignettes, and celebrity stories that fill this book describe Extreme Narcissists who were shaped by their painful childhoods. Abandonment or early loss of a parent, physical abuse, emotional neglect, exploitation in the service of parental narcissism, exposure to a parent's envy and hatred—the Extreme Narcissist is not "born that way" but is shaped by trauma. As you struggle to cope with the narcissist you know, feeling compassion for his shame may help you to avoid the winner-loser battleground.

Empathizing in such cases involves an act of emotional imagination: the very shame that might humanize the Extreme Narcissist is exactly what he does not want you to see. You'll need to infer its presence by recognizing the defenses against shame that by now have become familiar: *blame*, *contempt*, and *righteous indignation*. Even if you manage to feel some compassion for his suffering, don't expect him to feel grateful. Because shame makes the Extreme Narcissist feel like a loser, he usually does not want your compassion (although he may try to manipulate you by evoking your pity). He may experience you as condescending and superior. He may renew his assault on your self-esteem in order to escape from his own shame.

Rather than overtly expressing them, rely upon empathy and compassion to guide your own behavior in the face of probable hostility. You need to be "bigger" than the narcissist you know by doing what you think is best *for both of you*, despite opposition. Again, it helps to think of yourself as parent to a child who is throwing a temper tantrum. You may need to set appropriate limits and define expectations for acceptable behavior. You may need to say "no" to a child who then responds by saying "I hate you!" At the same time, you mustn't lose sight of the pain and shame concealed behind all that rage. According to Behary, coping with the narcissist you know involves a kind of reparenting—"nurturing the lonely and deprived child hidden within, doing so with both caring and guidance."[8]

I'm less optimistic than Behary about the healing potential of such reparenting; her cognitive-behavior approach sometimes strikes me as naïve. Core shame is a profound affliction, and the only chance for an Extreme Narcissist to heal in a real way is for him to face that shame. Feeling compassion in order to set limits and define expectations may help you to protect yourself, and even do the narcissist you know some limited and temporary good, but it does little to promote authentic growth in someone devoted to a *relentless narcissistic defense* (see Chapter Three).

DISENGAGE

Behary offers her guidance to a presumably female audience romantically involved with a male narcissist. While much of her advice might be useful, truly following it sounds like a Herculean chore with very little reward for all the effort. Why would you want to remain in a relationship where survival depends upon viewing your (ostensibly adult) partner as a child so beset by fear and shame that he can't reciprocate your concern? You might be able to limit his more destructive behaviors, but what exactly is your emotional reward? Despite your best efforts, he will remain largely incapable of true love and empathy.

When we cling to apparently unrewarding relationships with narcissistic partners, we usually do so for unhealthy (and unconscious) reasons. If we, too, struggle with shame, we might want to hold on to "the special way they make us feel when we are included in their

grandiosity." Like Winona, we might be reenacting an unhappy relationship with a narcissistic parent, hoping for a better outcome the
second time around. On an unconscious level, we may fear our own
needs and try to avoid true dependency by committing to a relationship where neediness is unsafe and best avoided. After all, conceiving
of a partner as a fearful, shame-ridden child makes the relationship
asymmetrical: Parents don't turn to their children in order to meet
their own needs.

When it comes to romantic involvements with an Extreme Narcissist, I believe your best course of action is to avoid them in the first
place, or to disengage once you realize their true nature. "Don't go
into a relationship with a narcissist thinking you are going to change
that person, or that he or she will change because of feelings for you.
Although people do sometimes change as a result of experiences in
relationships, this requires something that the narcissist lacks, the
capacity to respond to compassion with compassion."[9]

THERE IS RARELY AN UP SIDE TO ENGAGING

Walking away isn't always an option, however. Sometimes you have
no choice but to remain in a difficult relationship, be it with a family member, boss, co-worker, or social acquaintance. In those cases,
successfully coping with the narcissist you know again means remem-
bering that shame is always an issue. Extreme Narcissists continually
build and defend their sense of self in order to ward off unconscious
shame; for this reason, you must avoid wounding their fragile self-
esteem. Employees who challenged Steve Jobs's know-it-all narcissism sometimes earned his grudging respect, but more often he would
redouble his efforts to humiliate them and prove he knew better.

As I've said before, the approach I suggest might strike you as cowardly, but resolving conflict with the narcissist you know is not the time to stand on high principle. Truth and fairness mean nothing to the Extreme Narcissist; an appeal to his reason or sense of justice will get you nowhere. Unless you're a crusader like David Walsh, the journalist who doggedly pursued Lance Armstrong in an effort to expose his doping program (at great financial and emotional cost), you're better off avoiding direct confrontation. Don't call him out or challenge the lies he has told. Like Walsh, who was subjected to lawsuits for libel and a media assault on his character, you may provoke a vendetta for having dared to tell the truth.

As Hotchkiss notes, "Ordinary assertiveness techniques are often ineffective with narcissists, because they take it as an assault on their specialness, grandiosity, and entitlement."[10] She recommends that you "find the gentlest way possible to deliver your message and then deftly repair the shame."[11] Often this involves a massage to their ego, boosting their self-esteem in order to soften any criticism.

Again, behaving this way might make you feel insincere or dishonest, but as Dale Carnegie long ago noted, even fair and honest criticism will put most people (and not only the Extreme Narcissist) on the defensive when it wounds their "precious pride." Knowing that your criticism is accurate and deserved will give you small comfort when you find yourself under attack. Like the lawyer friend I described in Chapter Eight, your best course of action may be to "roll over" and thereby nip any attack in the bud. Of course, this requires a fairly strong sense of self and a belief in your own worth, without much external validation.

Sometimes this technique will also fail and nothing you do will be enough to mollify the Extreme Narcissist. He may feel your very existence as a kind of ongoing insult. Like Marie (see Chapter Three), who was the victim of workplace bullying, you may need to look for another job. As Tyler McOwen (in Chapter Nine) discovered, when you wound a Vindictive Narcissist, he will sometimes pursue revenge with an irrational, ruthless, and relentless drive no matter what you say or do. In those cases, keeping a written record of your interactions, documenting your own work, and seeking legal counsel may be necessary.

Tina Swithin kept a journal in which she recorded all of Seth's lies and breaches of their child custody agreement. She relied on a GPS tracking app installed on her daughters' cellphones to prove that Seth was in violation of that agreement. She kept recordings of all his phone messages to demonstrate to the court his abusive nature. At times, Swithin may have thought of her ex-husband as a small and frightened little boy throwing a temper tantrum, but compassion didn't undermine her hard-nosed realism about the need to defend herself legally.

In many cases, the Extreme Narcissist poses a dangerous threat, and you need to protect yourself by every means possible.

NARCISSISTIC CHILDREN: THE ONE SITUATION WHERE YOU CAN—AND MUST—SAY "NO"

In our families, an underperforming but Grandiose Narcissist like Shiloh (see Chapter Six) poses a different kind of problem. So does an Addicted Narcissist like my client Ian from the last chapter, who abandons us for a closer relationship with his drug. Addressing their insidious grandiosity requires different tactics, though shame is still the issue. The way they affect our self-esteem is more subtle, but we must again look to our own narcissistic vulnerabilities if we are to cope with them effectively.

Most couples like Anne and John, Shiloh's parents, feel anguished by their child's lack of motivation, self-centered indifference to the feelings of others, and apparent lack of a moral compass. "Where did we go wrong?" they wonder. "We were devoted parents, he had every advantage, and look how he turned out!" It may be difficult for them to acknowledge how they contributed to the problem. Because they wanted so desperately to rear a "winner" child in order to disprove their own shame, they continued to idealize him long past the time when his grandiosity needed a reality check. Instead of setting appropriate limits and realistic standards, they continued to praise everything he did and administer feeble, often meaningless punishments for misbehavior.

Parents aren't always to blame. Growing up in an era that encourages self-display and promotes a sense of entitlement undoubtedly contributes to the problem. In the more serious cases of slacker grandiosity, however, the root cause is often parental narcissism. While some Narcissistic Parents like Earl Woods or Joseph Jackson are so relentlessly perfectionistic that they drive their children to become overachievers, other parents like Anne and John idealize and indulge their children, treating them as if everything they do is (almost by definition) a major accomplishment. They want so badly to believe their child is *special* that they fail to teach the standards and self-discipline necessary for success.

Coping with such a child in later life requires the parents to own their role in creating the problem and to help their child face his shame. The Grandiose Narcissist with a powerful sense of entitlement may come across as superior or indifferent, but like my client Nicole, she feels herself to be a loser on an unconscious level. Arrogance and contempt usually disguise profound feelings of shame. Many parents continue to promote their children's defenses against shame well into adulthood by allowing them to live at home without contributing to the household, supporting them financially if they lead a superficially independent existence, or repeatedly rescuing them from emergencies. By protecting their sons and daughters from the consequences of their own choices, such parents make it difficult for their children to learn from their experience.

Even if your narcissistic child has reached adulthood, you need to apply widely accepted parenting strategies for dealing with younger children who act out. Learn to set appropriate limits and say "no." Define age-appropriate expectations and specify the consequences of failing to live up to them. Follow through with punishment and be consistent. When confronted with her sense of entitlement, sometimes expressed in the form of temper tantrums, don't be swayed by personal attacks. Don't expect your child to like you or be grateful. "Tough love" is a widely used and misunderstood parenting technique, but refusing to rescue your child from the consequences of her self-destructive behavior is often the most loving thing you can do. As difficult and painful as it may be, you sometimes need to let your children fail and fall hard.

If you continue to support your child's grandiosity and sense of entitlement, your own narcissism is at least partly to blame.

NARCISSISTIC ADDICTS: CHANGE YOURSELF, NOT THE ADDICT

Because the language of addiction permeates our culture and we've been taught to view it as a largely biochemical condition, understanding and coping with the Addicted Narcissist begins with a shift in perspective. Physiological dependence may be a fact, but it doesn't account for the grandiosity concealed within the addiction. Rather than viewing the addict's lack of concern for other people as a by-product of his addiction, we need to see it as a preexisting condition. Instead of viewing shame as simply the result of addictive behavior, we need to understand it as a contributing factor as well.

While twelve-step programs have their limitations, their methods implicitly address these factors. Acknowledging that one is powerless over an addiction and submitting oneself to a higher power curtails grandiosity. In their spiritual dimension, twelve-step programs view self-centeredness as the primary "spiritual malady," and the goal of working through the steps is to replace it with a new moral consciousness and concern for others. By facing the hurtful effects of one's past behavior and attempting to make amends for it, the addict places value on the feelings of those other people. In the process, bearing guilt and shame inevitably becomes a part of the recovery process.

If an Addicted Narcissist is a member of your family, or if you find yourself romantically involved with one, "you might as well beat your head against the wall as try to change them. If you want relief, you're going to have to change you." [12] As Hotchkiss notes, "People who are drawn to and remain in relationships with addicted and compulsive others are called co-dependents, and they usually have their own not-so-healthy reasons for needing to control or take care of those who are out of control." [13] CODA, or Co-Dependents Anonymous, is another twelve-step program that views co-dependency as but another form of addiction. Like other such recovery programs, it involves curtailing grandiosity and facing guilt and shame—in other words, confronting one's own narcissism. As I stated earlier, *co-narcissist* is a widely used synonym for *co-dependent*.

On a practical level, turning inward to deal with your own issues sometimes means breaking off a relationship with an Addicted Narcissist. At the very least, it means establishing new limits and better boundaries. Refuse to take part in or support any kind of addictive behavior—that is, don't *enable* the addiction by tolerating it in your presence or lending money to support the habit. Refuse to tolerate abusive behavior. Just as you might do with a child who acts out his grandiose sense of entitlement in self-destructive ways, stop rescuing him from the consequences of his behavior. You're not actually helping the Addicted Narcissist or taking care of yourself if you believe you can save him.

NARCISSISM EXISTS ON A CONTINUUM—WHERE ARE YOU?

In recent years, calling someone a narcissist has become a favorite way to express scorn. Reporters, pundits, and armchair psychologists regularly apply the label to other people as a way to mock or criticize them, to invalidate their political positions, or even to vent hatred. To take but one example: An Internet search for the term "Obama narcissist" returns hundreds of thousands of largely right-wing sites using pseudo-psychiatric analysis to attack the president.

While our society has grown increasingly compassionate toward those who suffer from mental illness, for the most part we don't extend that compassion to the Extreme Narcissist. A diagnosis of Narcissistic Personality Disorder makes the other person seem almost inhuman. Narcissists are villains—selfish and grandiose, incapable of fellow feeling, ruthlessly exploitative, brutal and vindictive, et cetera. In short, they are nothing like the rest of us, and we don't like them.

With its disease model of mental illness, the DSM also encourages us to view narcissism as a discrete disorder afflicting *those other difficult people*. Because media references to Narcissistic Personality Disorder so often sound like condemnation, you naturally want to set yourself apart from those who receive such a diagnosis. If you run down the symptoms checklist, expressed in the language of extremes, it's easy to overlook the ways in which you *sometimes* seem a little self-impressed; or how, *under certain conditions*, you lose empathy for the people you care about. You may not recognize your own occasional defenses when you hear them described as fixed character traits.

My primary aim in this book has been to place narcissism along a continuum of many possible expressions and to identify what we have in common with Extreme Narcissists rather than to emphasize our differences. This final chapter continues my theme, for coping effectively with the narcissist you know often means facing your own narcissistic vulnerabilities. When they wound your "precious pride" with their contempt, blame, or indignation, you may respond with similar narcissistic defenses in order to ward off feelings of shame and humiliation. Their boasting might provoke your envy because you, too, secretly long to be a winner. Or you may fall prey to their seductions for the same reason. You may collude with their addictions or support their dysfunctional lifestyles because the caretaker role allows you to avoid confronting your own shame.

In Chapter One, I recounted an experience where I had to face my own self-absorption and lack of concern for my piano teacher—that is, my own everyday sort of narcissism. I'd like to close with another, more painful anecdote, one that I hope will illustrate the complex interplay between narcissistic behavior in other people and our own defensive responses, often narcissistic in their own way. It took place at a dinner party many years ago when I still lived in Los Angeles, during a period when I was struggling to find my way as a writer.

Katie, one of the guests that evening, was a successful Hollywood writer and Emmy Award nominee. Smart, vivacious, and opinionated, she had a tendency to dominate conversations. She often talked at length about her frustrations as a sitcom writer while dropping references to the large amounts of money she made. She and her husband had recently purchased a new home in the Hollywood Hills for a high price she casually mentioned. At most social events where I'd met her, she usually found a way to bring up that Emmy Award nomination. In a much subtler, less offensive way than Monica, the Know-It-All Narcissist I described in Chapter Seven, Katie had a way of asserting her superiority.

Although I didn't quite realize it at the time, she also made me envious. For much of my life, I had longed for the life of a working, self-supporting writer. In many ways, Katie was living the life that I wanted. She also made me feel like a failure, though I know it wasn't her intention. On some level, I knew that Katie had worked more diligently at her craft than I had. I've spent many years since overcoming my defects as a writer, but back then, I felt ashamed (mostly on an unconscious level) that I hadn't undertaken the long, hard work.

At this dinner party, Katie was telling us about an argument with the head writer on her TV show. Her boss, an older male, wanted her to make changes to a script and she had refused. As their disagreement escalated, he called her some fairly rude and contemptuous names. He told her she had a "problem with authority." He said she needed to work out her "issues with men."

"I don't think I have issues with men," Katie said to the table at large. She'd had a lot to drink by this point and her speech was slightly slurred. "That's just his chauvinistic way of putting an uppity woman in her place. Men don't like strong women."

Anyone with psychological insight who knew Katie well could recognize that men in positions of authority consistently made her rebellious.

"Well, I for one *do* think you have issues with men," I told her.

It was a rude and hostile thing to say, though my tone was neutral. For a mental health professional speaking with some degree of expertise, it was almost cruel. To this day, I feel ashamed when I recall that evening.

Katie wasn't an Extreme Narcissist, though she had a tendency to think a little too well of herself. At social gatherings, she often asserted her superiority over other people in subtle ways, without much regard for their feelings. She was an everyday narcissist. I'm sure you've met many men and women like her.

Without quite acknowledging it to myself, I felt like a loser in comparison. Low-level boasting about her success as a writer incited my envy. As narcissists often do, she tapped into my own issues and challenged my self-esteem. In true narcissistic fashion, I then exploited my professional status to put her down. My comment had nothing to do with male chauvinism and all to do with my own shame. In order to boost my self-image, I humiliated her.

Do you have painful recollections like this one? Perhaps you have a memory you can't quite let go of; sometimes when it comes to mind, you tend to justify yourself in your own thoughts, as if trying to prove to an invisible third-party spectator that you have absolutely nothing to regret and no reason to feel guilty. The other person is to blame and deserved whatever she got. Such persistent memories and our defensive responses to them often point toward unconscious guilt and shame. Righteousness and blame, as I have shown, are narcissistic defenses that shore up a shaky sense of self.

It took me years to fully understand and acknowledge the reasons for my behavior. For a long time, I persuaded myself that I had only spoken the truth, denying that my words were colored by hostility. When I finally brought myself around to issuing an apology, it was half-hearted. Shame is an excruciating, often unbearable emotion to face. Had I understood myself better, I might have responded to Katie in ways that wouldn't have wounded her "precious pride" and preserved my own self-respect.

I offer this account to show how coping with the narcissist you know often means grappling with your own narcissistic vulnerabilities. When a self-styled winner makes you feel like a loser, you, too, may try to turn the tables in order to shore yourself up. You might behave in defensive ways that only make you feel worse about yourself later on. You might give voice to your envy or express yourself with contempt, all with a righteous sense of justification.

In short, coping with narcissistic traits in other people often means coming to terms with the narcissist you know the best but perhaps understand the least.

The one in your mirror.

ACKNOWLEDGMENTS

When I first thought about writing these acknowledgments, a book I often read to my three children came to mind. You may know it—*If You Give a Mouse a Cookie*. In this story, one action precipitates another in an unexpected but logical chain of events. Giving the mouse that cookie makes him thirsty, and so he asks for a glass of milk, and then a straw with which to drink it, and so on. The genesis of *The Narcissist You Know* strikes me as a long chain of events, one precipitating another, that led unexpectedly but inexorably to the book you have just finished reading.

My parents gave me life and provided me with a comfortable middle-class upbringing for which I am grateful, but if they hadn't done such a poor job on the emotional front, I would never have spent thirteen years on Michael Ian Paul's analytic couch. Dr. Paul literally saved my life and taught me most of what I know about the practice of psychotherapy. I would never have become a psychoanalyst if I hadn't been inspired by his fine example.

If I hadn't entered analytic training, I would never have become close friends with Tom Grant (who died long ago of kidney cancer) and his wife, Ann Glasser, also a psychoanalyst-in-training. During a crisis in my personal life many years later, Ann and I began to discuss what she was learning about shame from her mentor, Jim Oakland. After Tom died, Ann followed Dr. Oakland from Los Angeles to Seattle, where she opened a practice and eventually remarried. My many conversations with Ann about unconscious shame and the defenses against it revolutionized my personal and professional life. Dr. Oakland's ideas, as conveyed to me by Ann Glasser, profoundly influenced my work and lie at the heart of this book. It seems odd, to owe so very much to a man I met only once, years ago when he lived in Los Angeles.

If Tom were still alive and married to Ann, both of them practicing in Los Angeles, I would probably still be living there; we had a close friendship and strong professional ties, supporting each other's practice with referrals. Tom's death and Ann's relocation had a lot to do with my ultimate decision to leave Los Angeles and move my own family to Chapel Hill.

If I hadn't moved to Chapel Hill, I would never have joined Laurel Goldman's Thursday afternoon writers class, to which I have belonged for fifteen years. I would never have met the best writing teacher and the most sensitive and insightful group of writers I have ever known: Christina Askounis, Angela Davis-Gardner, Peter Filene, and Peggy Payne. As I worked my way through this book, these friends and fellow writers listened to me read every word. They lent their support and enthusiasm, contributed their often brilliant suggestions, and helped me to improve it immeasurably. I like to think of *The Narcissist You Know* as *our* achievement.

I originally set out to write a book about shame but was told by every literary agent I contacted that book editors wouldn't take to the idea. If I hadn't been universally turned down, I would never have changed course and written a book about narcissism instead. My oldest son, William, had been urging me for some time to write a book about celebrity narcissism.

If William hadn't also encouraged me to start blogging years earlier, one fateful day when we were hiking in Colorado, I would never have developed the Internet "platform" that gives me credibility with publishers and helped me land my contract with Touchstone Books.

If Michael Eha hadn't suggested I write an article about Lance Armstrong, it would never have occurred to me to use celebrity stories as a way to shed light on the psychology of narcissism.

If I hadn't hired my excellent publicist, Sharon Bially, to promote my earlier book *Why Do I Do That?*, I would never have been published in *The Atlantic*. When I wrote that article about Lance Armstrong, she introduced me to editor James Hamblin, who has published many of my articles in *The Atlantic*'s online health section.

If I hadn't written such a flawed novel years earlier, my former literary agent wouldn't have referred me to freelance book editor par excellence Emily Heckman, with whom I reconnected as I began drafting the proposal for this book in 2013. A former executive editor at Pocket Books and the co-author of some nine books, Emily was incisive in her critiques of the evolving proposal, creative in her suggestions, and enthusiastic in her support. She had a powerful role in shaping this book. In the process, she also became a close friend.

If literary agent Eric Nelson hadn't gotten the ball rolling by signaling early interest in my book proposal, and also offering his guidance in choosing among literary agents, I might never have signed with Gillian MacKenzie. Gillian is that rare combination of good

Acknowledgments

taste, strong writing skills, business acumen, and insight into what sells in the publishing world. She helped me refine the book proposal with her acute insights and marketing savvy. Her excellent assistant, Allison Devereux, is reliable, thorough, and a pleasure to work with.

If Michelle Howry hadn't been so enthusiastic about that proposal and acquired it for Touchstone Books, you wouldn't be holding my book in your hands today. Throughout the drafting and editing of the manuscript, Michelle was a gentle critic, wise guide, and enthusiastic supporter. She played a crucial role in shaping the book and refining its message. If she hadn't been my editor, my book would no doubt have been less successful.

If . . . if . . . if . . . I owe a debt of gratitude to all these people.

I'm also grateful to the clients who have entrusted themselves to my care over the years. I'd like to thank the excellent team at Simon & Schuster. I want to thank my "outside" readers who offered their praise and suggestions for early drafts of the manuscript: William Burgo, Lois Eha, Michael Eha, and Carolyn Fisher. My friends Dave Birkhead, Cady Erickson, Sue Jarrell, Sherry Kinlaw, Kathy Stanford, and Cathryn Taylor cheered me along throughout the writing process.

If I didn't have such a fine creative team and supportive friends at my side, I wouldn't be as proud and happy as I am today.

SUGGESTED READING

The professional literature on narcissism is vast. This short list includes the titles I find most helpful for an understanding of the psychodynamics of narcissism, with some titles offering guidance for the professional on treatment and others giving advice to laypersons for how to cope with the Extreme Narcissists in their lives.

Behary, Wendy T. *Disarming the Narcissist: Surviving & Thriving with the Self-Absorbed*. Oakland, CA: New Harbinger Publications, 2013.

Bradshaw, John. *Healing the Shame that Binds You*. Rev. ed. Deerfield Beach, FL: HCI, 2005.

Hotchkiss, Sandy. *Why Is It Always about You? The Seven Deadly Sins of Narcissism*. New York: Free Press, 2003.

Kernberg, Otto F. *Borderline Conditions and Pathological Narcissism*. New York: Jason Aronson, Inc., 1975.

Kohut, Heinz. *The Restoration of the Self*. New York: International Universities Press, Inc., 1997.

Masterson, James F. *The Narcissistic and Borderline Disorders: An Integrated Developmental Approach*. New York: Brunner/Mazel, 1981.

Miller, Alice. *The Drama of the Gifted Child*. New York: Basic Books, 1981; 2008.

Morrison, Andrew. *Shame: The Underside of Narcissism*. Hillsdale, NJ: The Atlantic Press, 1989.

Nathanson, Donald. *Shame and Pride: Affect, Sex and the Birth of the Self*. New York: W.W. Norton, Inc., 1992.

Schore, Allan. *Affect Regulation and the Origin of the Self: The Neurobiology of Emotional Development*. Hillsdale, NJ: Erlbaum, 1994.

ENDNOTES

2.
"I'M EASILY WOUNDED": SELF-ESTEEM AND NARCISSISTIC INJURY

1. Dale Carnegie, *How to Win Friends and Influence People* (1936; reprint, New York: Simon & Schuster, 2009), 5.
2. Andrew Morrison, *Shame: The Underside of Narcissism* (Hillsdale, NJ: The Atlantic Press, 1989).

3.
"I'M A WINNER AND YOU'RE A LOSER": THE BULLYING NARCISSIST

1. Otto F. Kernberg, *Borderline Conditions and Pathological Narcissism* (New York: Jason Aronson, Inc., 1975), 234.
2. Anna Freud, *The Ego and the Mechanisms of Defense* (New York: International Universities Press, Inc., 1946).
3. D. W. Winnicott, "The basis for self in body," in *Psycho-Analytic Explorations*, ed. C. Winnicott, R. Shepherd, and M. Davis (London: Karnac, 1989).
4. John Bradshaw, *Healing the Shame that Binds You*, rev. ed. (Deerfield Beach, FL: HCI, 2005).
5. Linda Armstrong Kelly, *No Mountain High Enough* (New York: Broadway Books, 2000), 19.
6. Reed Albergotti and Vanessa O'Connell, *Wheelmen* (New York: Dutton, 2013), 39.
7. Lance Armstrong and Sally Jenkins, *It's Not about the Bike* (New York: Putnam, 2000).

8. http://www.workplacebullying.org/individuals/problem/who-gets-targeted.
9. http://www.bullyingstatistics.org/content/bullying-and-suicide.html/.

4.

"YOU'RE EVERYTHING I ALWAYS/NEVER WANTED TO BE": THE NARCISSISTIC PARENT

1. Allan Schore, *Affect Regulation and the Origin of the Self: The Neurobiology of Emotional Development* (Hillsdale, NJ: Lawrence Erlbaum Associates, 1994).
2. Alice Miller, *The Drama of the Gifted Child* (New York: Basic Books, 1981; 2008), 5–7.
3. *Ibid.*, 8.
4. Tom Callahan, *His Father's Son: Earl and Tiger Woods* (New York: Gotham Books, 2010), 6.
5. *Ibid.*
6. *Ibid.*
7. *Ibid.*, 4.
8. *Ibid.*, 4–5.
9. *Ibid.*, 15.
10. *Ibid.*, 13.
11. *Ibid.*, 17.
12. *Ibid.*, 41.
13. *Ibid.*, 45.
14. http://www.si.com/vault/1996/12/23/220709/the-chosen-tiger-woods.
15. Callahan, *His Father's Son*, 44.
16. *Ibid.*, 232.
17. http://www.denverpost.com/sports/ci_12111710.
18. http://www.nydailynews.com/news/tiger-woods-press-conference-transcript-full-text-apology-article-1.195565.
19. http://www.tmz.com/2010/04/02/tiger-woods-kindergarten-teacher-racism-gloria-allred-liar-ms-decker/.
20. Callahan, *His Father's Son*, 96.
21. By focusing on narcissistic mothers, I don't mean to suggest that women are more narcissistic than men as parents. They're not. But despite the greater role fathers have recently come to play in the lives of their babies, mothers still tend to have a greater influence during the earliest years. Narcissistic fathers often abandon their families, too, neglecting their responsibilities in the pursuit of self-gratification. They injure their children through neglect, but it is a less directly pernicious effect than the damage caused by narcissistic mothers.

Endnotes

5.
"I WANT YOU TO WANT ME": THE SEDUCTIVE NARCISSIST

1. http://www.huffingtonpost.com/2013/08/08/bill-clinton_n_3718956.html.
2. Tina Swithin, *Divorcing a Narcissist: One Mom's Battle* (San Luis Obispo, CA: Self-Published, 2012), 11.
3. *Ibid.*, 20.
4. Donald Nathanson, *Shame and Pride: Affect, Sex, and the Birth of the Self* (New York: W.W. Norton, Inc., 1992).
5. J. Randy Taraborrelli, *Madonna: An Intimate Biography* (New York: Simon & Schuster, 2001), 13.
6. Kernberg, *Borderline Conditions*, 235.
7. Taraborrelli, *Madonna*, 8.
8. *Ibid.*, 52.
9. *Ibid.*, 66.
10. *Ibid.*, 82.
11. *Ibid.*, 82–83.
12. *Ibid.*, 57.
13. *Ibid.*, 66.
14. *Ibid.*, 67.
15. *Ibid.*, 23.
16. John Skow, "Madonna Rocks the Land," *Time*, May 27, 1985, 7.
17. Max Weber, *The Theory of Social and Economic Organization*, trans. A. M. Henderson and Talcott Parsons (Glencoe: Free Press, 1947), 358.
18. Swithin, *Divorcing a Narcissist*, 19.

6.
"I'M KING OF THE WORLD": THE GRANDIOSE NARCISSIST

1. http://www.nytimes.com/2013/06/16/arts/music/kanye-west-talks-about-his-career-and-album-yeezus.html?pagewanted=all&_r=0.
2. Jean M. Twenge and W. Keith Campbell, *The Narcissism Epidemic: Living in the Age of Entitlement* (New York: Atria Books, 2009).
3. *Ibid.*
4. Brad J. Bushman and Roy F. Baumeister, "Threatened egotism, narcissism, self-esteem, and direct and displaced aggression: Does self-love or self-hate lead to violence?" in *Journal of Personality and Social Psychology* (1998, vol. 75, no. 1), 219–229.
5. http://en.wikipedia.org/wiki/Mister_Peabody#cite_note-MPSStoryOverlay-1.

Endnotes

6. Drew Pinsky and S. Mark Young, *The Mirror Effect: How Celebrity Narcissism Is Seducing America* (New York: HarperCollins, 2009), 15.

7. Jake Halpern, *Fame Junkies: The Hidden Truths behind America's Favorite Addiction* (New York: Houghton Mifflin Harcourt, 2007).

8. Daniel Joseph Boorstin, *The Image: A Guide to Pseudo-Events in America* (New York: Vintage, 1961).

9. Joseph Burgo, *The Hero as Narcissist: How Lance Armstrong and Greg Mortenson Conned a Willing Public* (Chapel Hill: New Rise Press, 2013).

10. http://www.lrb.co.uk/v36/n05/andrew-ohagan/ghosting.

11. http://www.newyorker.com/reporting/2010/06/07/100607fa_fact_khatchadourian?currentPage=all.

12. O'Hagan, *Ghosting*.

13. http://www.independent.co.uk/news/uk/home-news/julian-assange-i-am-ndash-like-all-hackers-ndash-a-little-bit-autistic-2358654.html.

14. Daniel Domscheit-Berg, *Inside WikiLeaks: My Time with Julian Assange at the World's Most Dangerous Website* (New York: Crown, 2011).

15. O'Hagan, *Ghosting*.

16. http://www.nytimes.com/2011/01/30/magazine/30Wikileaks-t.html?pagewanted=all&_r=0.

7.
"I HAVE SO MUCH TO TELL YOU": THE KNOW-IT-ALL NARCISSIST

1. Martha Stout, *The Sociopath Next Door: The Ruthless versus the Rest of Us* (New York: Broadway Books, 2005), 60.

2. *Ibid.*, 92.

3. http://www.vanityfair.com/style/scandal/2014/01/bikram-choudhury-yoga-sexual-harassment.

4. *Ibid.*

5. *Ibid.*

6. Walter Isaacson, *Steve Jobs* (New York: Simon & Schuster, 2011), 118.

7. *Ibid.*

8. *Ibid.*, 120.

9. *Ibid.*, 119.

10. *Ibid.*

11. http://www.esquire.com/features/second-coming-of-steve-jobs-1286.

12. Isaacson, *Steve Jobs*, 121.

13. *Ibid.*, 12.

14. *Ibid.*, 246.

Endnotes

15. *Ibid.*, 264–265.
16. *Ibid.*, 266.
17. *Ibid.*, 5.
18. *Ibid.*, 257.
19. *Ibid.*
20. Nancy Newton Verrier, *The Primal Wound: Understanding the Adopted Child* (Baltimore: Gateway Press, 2003), 1.
21. O. Kernberg, "Pathological narcissism and narcissistic personality disorder: Theoretical background and diagnostic classification," in E. F. Ronningstam (ed.), *Disorders of Narcissism: Diagnostic, Clinical, and Empirical Implications* (Washington, DC: American Psychiatric Press, 1998), 29–51.

8.
"I'M RIGHT AND YOU'RE WRONG": THE SELF-RIGHTEOUS NARCISSIST

1. Nathanson, *Shame and Pride*, 128.
2. *Ibid.*, 129.
3. http://www.vanityfair.com/hollywood/features/2011/03/mel-gibson-201103.
4. *Ibid.*
5. *Ibid.*
6. http://www.deadline.com/2011/04/exclusive-mel-gibson-finally-talks/.
7. http://gawker.com/5593265/mel-gibsons-phone-rants-the-complete-collection.
8. Martin Kantor, "Coping, containing, and countering antigay prejudice and discrimination," in Jean Lau Chin (ed.), *The Psychology of Prejudice and Discrimination (Race and Ethnicity in Psychology)* (New York: Praeger, 2004), 227.
9. N. Weinstein et al., "Parental autonomy support and discrepancies between implicit and explicit sexual identities: Dynamics of self-acceptance and defense," in *Journal of Personality and Social Psychology*, vol. 102(4), April 2012, 815–832.
10. http://gawker.com/5533901/second-gay-escort-claims-sexual-encounter-with-george-rekers.
11. Gwenda Blair, *Donald Trump, Master Apprentice* (New York: Simon & Schuster, 2005), 18.
12. *Ibid.*, 84.
13. *Ibid.*, 11.
14. *Ibid.*, 13.
15. *Ibid.*, 4.

16. *Ibid.*, 31.

17. *Ibid.*, 215.

18. *Ibid.*, 174.

19. *Ibid.*, 135.

20. *Ibid.*, 197.

21. *Ibid.*, 116.

22. John. R. O'Donnell with James Rutherford, *Trumped! The Inside Story of the Real Donald Trump—His Cunning Rise and Spectacular Fall* (New York: Simon & Schuster, 1991), 54–55.

23. *Ibid.*, 70.

24. *Ibid.*, 326.

9.
"CHALLENGE ME AND I'LL HURT YOU": THE VINDICTIVE NARCISSIST

1. A montage of his more famous outbursts is available on YouTube, https://www.youtube.com/watch?v=koE_e_LX4c0.

2. Swithin, *Divorcing a Narcissist*, 63.

3. *Ibid.*, 64.

4. *Ibid.*, 116–117.

5. *Ibid.*, 135.

6. *Ibid.*, 230.

7. *Ibid.*, 231.

8. *Ibid.*, 218.

9. Geoffrey Dunn, *The Lies of Sarah Palin: The Untold Story behind Her Relentless Quest for Power* (New York: St. Martin's Press, 2011), 23.

10. http://www.vanityfair.com/politics/features/2009/08/sarah-palin200908?printable=true&currentPage=all.

11. Sarah Palin, *Going Rogue: An American Life* (New York: HarperCollins, 2009).

12. Dunn, *Lies of Sarah Palin*, 38–39.

13. Joe McGinnis, *The Rogue: Searching for the Real Sarah Palin* (New York: Crown, 2011), 19–20.

14. Dunn, *Lies of Sarah Palin*, 38.

15. *Ibid.*, 39.

16. McGinnis, *Rogue*, 19.

17. *Ibid.*, 20.

18. *Ibid.*, 28.

19. *Ibid.*, 28–29.

20. *Ibid.*, 29.

21. *Ibid.*, 84.
22. *Ibid.*, 131.
23. *Ibid.*, 132.
24. Dunn, *Lies of Sarah Palin*, 62.
25. *Ibid.*, 62–63.
26. *Ibid.*, 65.
27. *Ibid.*, 71.
28. *Ibid.*, 74.
29. *Ibid.*, 75.
30. *Ibid.*
31. McGinnis, *Rogue*, 91.
32. *Ibid.*, 92.
33. Dunn, *Lies of Sarah Palin*, 109.
34. *Ibid.*
35. *Ibid.*, 248.
36. *Ibid.*, 131.
37. McGinnis, *Rogue*, 143.
38. *Ibid.*, 144–145.
39. John Heilemann and Mark Helperin, *Game Change: Obama and the Clintons, McCain and Palin, and the Race of a Lifetime* (New York: HarperCollins, 2010), 400–404.
40. *Ibid.*, 400.
41. Swithin, *Divorcing a Narcissist*, 231.
42. *Ibid.*, 257.

10.
"MY DRUG MEANS MORE TO ME THAN YOU DO": THE ADDICTED NARCISSIST

1. Nathanson, *Shame and Pride*, 355.
2. *Ibid.*
3. *Ibid.*
4. *Ibid.*, 356.
5. *Ibid.*
6. Otto Fenichel, *The Psycho-Analytic Theory of Neuroses* (New York: Norton, 1974), 377.
7. S. J. Blatt, et al., "The psychodynamics of opiate addiction," in *The Journal of Nervous and Mental Disease*, vol. 172, no. 6 (June, 1984):342–352.
8. Philip J. Flores, *Addiction as an Attachment Disorder* (New York: Jason Aaronson, 2004), 81.

Endnotes

9. *Ibid.*

10. Heinz Kohut, *The Restoration of the Self* (New York: International Universities Press, Inc., 1977), 197, n. 11.

11. https://uk.news.yahoo.com/plastic-surgery-addict-spends-%C2%A3100k-to-look-like-ken-doll-130450501.html#KDuJmvc.

12. Ibid.

13. J. Randy Taraborrelli, *Michael Jackson: The Magic, the Madness, the Whole Story, 1958–2009* (New York: Grand Central, 2009), 20.

14. *Ibid.*, 20–21.

15. Randall Sullivan, *Untouchable: The Strange Life and Tragic Death of Michael Jackson* (New York: Grove Press, 2012), 41.

16. *Ibid.*, p. 66.

17. Taraborrelli, *Michael Jackson*, 205.

18. *Ibid.*

19. *Ibid.*, 177–178.

20. *Ibid.*, 230.

21. *Ibid.*, 231–232.

22. Sullivan, *Untouchable*, 271.

23. *Ibid.*, 270.

24. Taraborrelli, *Michael Jackson*, 567.

25. *Ibid.*, 472.

26. Sullivan, *Untouchable*, 119.

27. Taraborrelli, *Michael Jackson*, 415.

28. Sullivan, *Untouchable*, 119.

29. *Ibid.*, 213.

30. *Ibid.*, 201.

31. *Ibid.*, 114.

32. *Ibid.*, 245.

33. Taraborrelli, *Michael Jackson*, 518.

34. *Ibid.*

35. Sullivan, *Untouchable*, 196.

36. Taraborrelli, *Michael Jackson*, 191.

11.
"I'M DIFFICULT BUT NOT IMPOSSIBLE TO MANAGE": COPING WITH THE NARCISSIST YOU KNOW

1. Sandy Hotchkiss, *Why Is It Always about You? The Seven Deadly Sins of Narcissism* (New York: Free Press, 2003), 61.

Endnotes

2. *Ibid.*, 62.
3. *Ibid.*
4. *Ibid.*, 63.
5. *Ibid.*, 67.
6. *Ibid.*
7. Wendy T. Behary, *Disarming the Narcissist: Surviving & Thriving with the Self-Absorbed* (Oakland: New Harbinger Publications, 2013), 148.
8. *Ibid.*
9. Hotchkiss, *Why Is It Always about You?*, 73.
10. *Ibid.*, 79.
11. *Ibid.*
12. *Ibid.*, 117.
13. *Ibid.*

ABOUT THE AUTHOR

Joseph Burgo has been a practicing psychotherapist and psychoanalyst for more than thirty years. He lives in Colorado and provides face-to-face video psychotherapy through a secure online platform to clients in Europe, Asia, and Africa, as well as throughout North America.